DURABLE
SUCCESS

DURABLE SUCCESS

EMPOWERED MANAGEMENT AND VISIONARY LEADERSHIP

A. Ovy Lungu

iUniverse, Inc.
New York Lincoln Shanghai

Durable Success
Empowered Management and Visionary Leadership

Copyright © 2005 by A. Ovy Lungu

iUniverse books may be ordered through booksellers or by contacting:

iUniverse
2021 Pine Lake Road, Suite 100
Lincoln, NE 68512
www.iuniverse.com
1-800-Authors (1-800-288-4677)

ISBN-13: 978-0-595-37540-0 (pbk)
ISBN-13: 978-0-595-81934-8 (ebk)
ISBN-10: 0-595-37540-5 (pbk)
ISBN-10: 0-595-81934-6 (ebk)

Printed in the United States of America

Many heartfelt thanks to all those who encouraged me to embark on this mission:

- *My guiding light, Letitia, who came up with a great cover design idea, and who supported, motivated and cheered me up all the way through*

- *My parents, Ovidiu Sr. (Magnum) and Elena, whose moral and material support was priceless*

- *My great mentor and friend John Kelly, who opened the door and allowed me to take a peek at the fascinating world of business management and leadership*

I'll forever be in your debt.

CONTENTS:

Prologue 1

Chapter I—Business Fundamentals .17
- The Functions of a Business 20
- Typical Business Organization .22

Chapter II—Introduction to Management 26
- Personal Stage 29
- Interpersonal Stage 32
- Managerial Stage 33
- Organizational Stage 34
- Level V leadership 36
- Manager's effectiveness 38
- Proactive Zone 39
- Fluctuating Zone 41
- Reactive Zone 42
- Destructive Zone 42
- The Strategic Plan in Management 47
- Customer Satisfaction Objectives 50
- Operational Effectiveness Objectives 51
- Financial Performance Objectives 55
- Marketing Objectives 56

Chapter III—Management one-on-one 58
- Key ingredients in management 58
- Plan 59
- Organize 70
- Direct 72
- Control 74
- Front Line Management 77
- The Overall Quality Management Model 89

Chapter IV—Customer Service 96
- Customer Expectations 101
- Value-Added Service 103
- The Difference between Expectations and Needs 106
- Needs 107
- Body Language 113
- How to Use Body Language to Diffuse Anger 119

Chapter V—Human Needs and Team Members 120
- Job Enlargement and Enrichment 121
- Peak Performance 123
- Preventing Performance Problems 126

Chapter VI—Acquiring the Leadership Perspective 133
- Competitive and Compound Value of Leadership 133
- Leadership Scale 137
- The follower 140
- Action Level 145

- Control Level 147
- Personal Level 151
- Interpersonal Level 156
- Empowerment Level 163
- Level V Leadership 167

Chapter VII—Creating Excellence and Repeated Success . . .169
- Excellence 169
- Activity Integration 199
- Primary Activities 200
- Support Activities 201
- Value Chain 202
- Operational Efficiency Activities 213
- Strategy 215

Epilogue 227

Acknowledgements 233

PROLOGUE

"Management is doing things right; leadership is doing the right things"

Peter F. Druckner, American Management Guru

The Art of Management…is this euphemism or is it reality? Some people were born leaders, with anything they touch or do turning into success overnight. The rest of us need to work hard at it, making progress in baby steps.

Throughout "DURABLE SUCCESS", the author intends to provide assistance in the quest for management, leadership and excellence by offering a foundation for anyone who contemplates advancement in the management field. In today's service-oriented economy training the team members is paramount to the long-term success of any company, and savvy managers pride themselves in deploying clever methods for training their staff using innovative thinking, modeled after great contemporary thinkers and leaders.

"DURABLE SUCCESS" is based on two models: one is a *leadership model* in which the focus is to become an example or benchmark of leadership; the other is a *management model*, designed to pay equal attention to four major areas of responsibility in business operations and development. By balancing the efforts and focus on these four areas any business can create long term growth and long-lasting success. "DURABLE SUCCESS" constitutes a self-improving and personal developing tool for new and seasoned team members alike, helping build the skills and knowledge to fulfill the targets of a satisfying management position. Too often people are hired or promoted

1

in management positions in haste and without much research, on a "warm body" principle, to quickly fill a need or void. Assuming that one's previous success in a lower or parallel capacity is the assurance for future job performance is akin to stealing your own hat. It opens up the door for a long and frustrating relationship unless the new hire or the recently promoted person is provided with all the tools necessary to make the quantum leap into the new management field. "DURABLE SUCCESS" provides just that—a means of creating new or honing the existing skills that modern managers ought to have in their arsenal. It will allow managers to abandon the "top-down" pyramidal method of running things. It introduces the concept of empowerment and encourages the modern management to challenge the status-quo and to find better and innovative ways to achieve results.

Unfortunately, in the management field dinosaurs still exist, who feel comfortable within the status-quo, and for whom any change presents an insurmountable obstacle. "DURABLE SUCCESS" is written with the hope to herd the relics of the management's past into the sunset by allowing fresh and proven successful management ideas to enter the playing field.

Chapter I presents a succinct overview of the business organization, on the credence that in order to understand management and leadership in today's business climate, first we need to understand what modern businesses are and how they operate. Chapter I explains what businesses do and describes various types of businesses. It outlines business functions and succinctly describes how they are organized. It does not pretend to be an exhaustive presentation of business organization but only a succinct reiteration of basic principles that most managers already have a grasp on.

Chapter II of the manual introduces the basics of management training. The legendary Lee Iacocca said "*Management is nothing more than motivating other people"* and training is the quintessential factor in the long-term success of any company. The great leaders of contemporary economic organizations strive to introduce innovative thinking and ideas in training methods to enable the wide range of management personnel to succeed.

As we delve into the challenging and more often than not very rewarding world of management, we need to first get a "bird's eye view" of the models that will be used throughout this text, which will allow the achievement of excellence. The first is an **Overall Quality Model** which employs sound business practices and naturally drives quality inside any domain it is applied: family, business endeavor, school, non-profit organization, and so on. It consists of five stages: **Personal Development, Interpersonal Skills Development, Managerial Development, Organizational Development**, and **Level V Leadership**.

The other model used herein is the **Equilibrium Square**, intended to attribute equal attention to the main four areas of responsibility of a service business: *Customer Relations and Satisfaction, Operational Effectiveness, Financial Performance* and *Marketing*. By balancing the efforts in these areas any service business will achieve long-term growth and profitability.

Chapter II also attempts to provide an answer to the question "What does it mean to be effective?" As an individual, as a manager or as a company we want to be effective. We want to become a model or reference in our field and this can't be achieved by just doing an OK job, barely bumping along. We can't create excellence out of mediocrity. Creating excellence is possible only by becoming highly effective people in whatever we do. Highly effective people are those who enhance their proactive skills, those who plan and organize instead of reacting and hiding from the truth.

Furthermore the author describes the four activity stages: Proactive, Fluctuating, Reactive and Destructive. Subsequently Chapter II presents the activities directly associated with each of these stages: *important but not urgent, not important but urgent, important and urgent, not important and not urgent.* We can figure out where we are by just looking at the majority of our activities that make up our day. This way we can figure out in which zone we operate.

Knowing where we are and what path to take to achieve greatness in a good start. For that we also need a strategic plan. Understanding this strategic plan helps aspiring managers in setting their own short term plans in order to achieve the company's long term plans. Also it helps identifying opportunities. Savvy managers can set their short term goals to fall within this area that creates a competitive advantage, making themselves more valuable to their organization.

The Equilibrium Square allows managers to impart equal attention and an equal degree of importance to all of its four areas by achieving and maintaining the following objectives:

- Customer Satisfaction: create win-win partnerships, create value-added services, and be perceived by the customer as the standard of excellence;

- Operational Effectiveness: create Overall Quality Management all throughout the company. Increase training and learning of the service industry's principles and the Overall Quality Model norms by developing team members, empower team members, provide the access to technology at all necessary levels that increase productivity and service quality, and cultivate and promote company's culture of discipline;

- Financial Performance: reduce operational costs, and make a minimum of x% profit;

- Marketing: increase exposure in the targeted markets, and create turbo growth by maximizing opportunities.

It's all about balance. Adding more accountability and attention to one area's performance without increasing the others leads to imbalance and frustration, not to mention that it will lead to the eventual collapse of the business.

Chapter III is dedicated to Management 101. Along with the responsibilities implied by accepting any job there are some fundamental components to all management positions. These components will determine the attitude of advancement in management career and the altitude of success. The purpose of management is to: Plan, Organize, Direct and Control. Each of these aspects is discussed in detail in the subchapter called "Key ingredients to management". These key ingredients offer a ground-up view of what management calls for.

Planning is one area that is discussed in detail in Part II. There are basically three types of planning and scores of savvy managers from sophisticated and highly successful Fortune 500 companies are engaged in them. They are: Operational Planning, Tactical Planning, and Strategic Planning.

Any service company is as good as its front line managers because these managers are the interface with the client. They project the company's values, strategy and way of thinking. That's why the front line managers' training is so important. The front line manager in a service-oriented business is the facilitator. The managers in this category facilitate the following two aspects of their job duties:

- The fulfillment of the company's tactical plan in accordance with established long term strategy set forth by the company's executive leadership.
- Creation and growth of an Overall Quality Management environment.

To facilitate these two areas means that front line managers have to help their associates, their distributors and their customers align their goals and actions with fulfilling the long-term plans and in the same time to establish an Overall Quality Model environment in their area of activity and responsibility. It means inoculating these goals into the prevention cycle so that front line managers are planning, organizing, directing and controlling the actions that lead to achieving their goals. Any discussion on front line management responsibilities needs to address three factors that make or break a service company: *the customer, the team members and the budget.* Each of these factors is subsequently discussed individually, introducing the concept of "value-added service" which translates into becoming customer-oriented.

Like the customer end of the equation, which is the subject of Part III, an equal amount of attention needs to be conferred to forming self-directed teams. Managers should think of team members as customers. If they are perceived that way managers will work just as hard to retain them.

Managers therefore provide *training and certification, motivation*, and *empowerment.* Empowerment is the opportunity to act instead of being acted upon. It's the freedom to select choices and make decisions; to take on responsibility and authority; to be allowed self-reliance and to be involved in decision-making that affect the environment.

Managers are also *providers* of the necessities that their teams require to be successful in their job. Besides job satisfiers, the team members need to be provided with the *tools and equipment* that make their work easier. Failure to fulfill this responsibility undermines all of the motivational techniques used. Another important responsibility of front line management is the creating, controlling and organizing the Work Schedule, which needs to shadow the schedule of all the working teams that are managed—leaving enough time during the normal business hours for administrative chores, for completing paperwork or for running errands.

The Overall Quality Management model is a long term management style that focuses on quality, empowerment and customer service. Overall Quality Model involves everyone in the organization and uses means of measurement to monitor team activity for continuous progress. Overall Quality Model changes attitudes and adjusts the way people are perceived. An Overall Quality Model style respects the dignity of human beings. The Overall Quality Model puts everyone on a level playing field so that intimidation is eliminated and nothing can smother creativity and innovation.

There are four fundamental components that act as a base of the Overall Quality Model. These ingredients allow for an environment where everyone in the organization can truly reach peak performance, creating an organization that is dedicated to quality and customer satisfaction. Consequently, the effects of creating an Overall Quality Model environment could be: reduced costs, competitive edge, improved effectiveness, improved customer satisfaction and increased revenue.

Chapter IV is dedicated to understanding customer service. Interacting successfully with customers requires artful skills. The art of customer service is no secret—it is simply the ability to influence people. When talking about influencing people, we step out of the management boundaries and enter the leadership zone.

In management mode we think "*be efficient*". To do so we use as reference the objects of our trade (budgets, time, tasks, etc.). To extrapolate, management is the art of being efficient with *objects*. However, if we apply a management perspective when interacting with people, we may be efficient in handling a situation. But dealing with people is totally different than dealing with things, because things don't come with emotions or core human needs. The key is to be *effective* with people. Being effective takes time. A leadership perspective pays the price to build relationships of trust, in order to influence people. Leaders always think first about how they can influence others. Only after that they start thinking in terms of time and efficiency.

To create win-win partnerships with the customer requires the knowledge of how to effectively meet core human needs. This is dependent upon the ability to use good people skills. Otherwise a partnership will never synergize.

Excellent customer service evolves from:

1. **Perfect inter-personal skills** that spring from principles like integrity, honesty and kindness.

2. **Meeting and maintaining customer's core human needs.** People will trust you more if they perceive that you are looking out for their best interest.

3. **Exceeding expectations.** This ability creates satisfaction and confidence.

4. **Building character.** Principles like integrity, honesty, kindness and others must be at your own core.

The author reveals two principles that can be used to exceed expectations: *the principle of overwhelming* and *the principle of small things.* "DURABLE SUCCESS" explains also the difference between expectations and needs. While expectations are rooted in the conscious mind, the needs come from a much deeper source—the subconscious mind. Therefore, needs are more universal than expectations to all human beings because the needs affect our self-identities or our sense of self-worth. Knowing human psychology and behavior can help build enduring relationships. It also helps in influencing people to do things because they want to do them. Used the right way this knowledge helps increase effectiveness and productivity in management. Furthermore, the author introduces the reader to the hierarchy of human needs according to psychologist Abraham Maslow who studied exemplary people such as Eleanor Roosevelt, Albert Einstein, and Frederick Douglas.

According to Maslow, there are general types of "deficiency needs" that must be satisfied before a person can act unselfishly. As long as we are motivated to satisfy these cravings, we are moving towards growth, toward self-actualization.

Chapter V is dedicated to the team members; how to fulfill their human needs in order to influence them. Here, the author explains that people are motivated through the fulfillment of needs. If you violate the needs of your team members, you will lose them in productivity, in ownership, in independence and eventually in employment.

Everyone has the ability to move up in the stages of need fulfillment. Unlocking someone's desires and will is the key to motivation. True motivation comes from the individual; we can't motivate anyone outright, we can only provide *keys* for motivation. For managers, these keys represent the way they treat their people and the environment they create for their teams. If they treat their teammates with respect, trust, competency and intelligence, most of the teammates will act with respect, trust, competency and intelligence.

The ultimate goal of management is to bring the team to peak performance and afterwards to prevent performance problems. We must understand what it means to perform. Similar to other things in life, we often do not seem to notice something as general as performance until we consider that there is a gap between what we perceive to be good performance and what we encounter. Everyone has different expectations for performance. There seems to be a fine line between *excessive performance* and *not enough*. How can we tell what peak performance is, or how do we tell if there's excessive or not enough performance? The answer is found in what is universally accepted as standards of performance. The standards impose a level that everyone must meet in order to achieve the optimum level of performance. There are two types of standards: they are *general* and *specific*.

The managers' goal is to prevent performance problems before they occur. Chapter V contains a Peak Performance Flowchart that can be used in preventing and responding to problems. The level of implementation of the material presented about peak performance will determine the level of productivity, turnover and loyalty achieved by each manager and if it all leads to happier work environments and a heftier bottom line.

Chapter VI explores the process of acquiring a leadership perspective through creating competitive and compounding value. The added value that *a leader*, as opposite to *a manager* creates is called *competitive value* and is defined as the quantity and quality of people and ideas created by the leadership.

When talking about people within an organization, competitive value refers to the sum of each individual's skills, talent, knowledge and attitudes plus all the other personal values brought in. For an organization, competitive value means the totality of the talent, work processes, strategies, and business activities that the organization possesses or engages in.

Nobody can create competitive value with a management perspective. A management perspective causes narrow thinking process, down to efficiency and expediency. The management perspective is inherently short-term thinking.

Leadership is a combination of a multitude of things but for simplicity's sake the author considers only the most important aspects:

- ❖ Leadership is self-improving and self-developing
- ❖ Leadership is constantly developing and preparing others
- ❖ Leadership constantly promotes vision and empowers others to greatness

Leadership either comes from natural abilities or through a learning process. Creating something from nothing is not possible in leadership. Everyone has to develop their skills, even those who have natural abilities into leadership. So what is a leader? Being in the lead is not enough. Many managers who are in a lead position are still not leaders, for management and leadership are not completely separate from one another. Management without any leadership is entirely possible; but conversely, you can't have leadership without a dose of management. Management in its pure state represents the early stage of leadership.

Starting from a leadership scale which depicts the evolution stages in the process of becoming a leader, the author assembles a leadership model which includes five levels. The follower, who represents "ground zero", can evolve to the action and control levels, which represent the management domain mentioned before. Beyond that it is the leadership domain which encompasses the personal level, the interpersonal level and the empowerment level. The pinnacle of leadership is "Level V" which requires the embodiment of a paradoxical mix of personal humility and professional strong will. Leaders at this level are dedicated first and foremost for the good of the company, not for themselves; they are almost fanatically driven to produce sustained results. It may be easy by just looking at the leadership model to say that someone has all the attributes listed under the levels of leadership. However, each attribute is composed of many different qualities and actions. Success lies in understanding the details. The Leadership Model provides only generalities. A closer look will help assess someone's own true strengths and weaknesses. Understanding all these steps helps with managers' self-evaluation of their position on the model scale, and at the same time will help determine if there's any competitive and compound value created for the employing organization. Nobody can mentor people in becoming Level V leaders; this is where individual grit and resolve determines the outcome. Level V leaders are not greater-than-life personalities who are easy to spot and so we may have a hard time finding a model to follow to achieve Level V. The secret is in observing the astounding results that the organizations, under Level V leadership are able to consistently and repeatedly produce.

The author attempts to dispel in Chapter VII the myths of creating excellence and enduring success. If a company sets its own standard of excellence, it translates in an atmosphere of competition only if the leaders and their teammates consider the standard too low and consequently, they collectively go all-out to elevate it. Variations in standards make it difficult for individuals and companies to determine the value they are supposed to generate. Having a standard to measure value against can help companies and individuals know what kind of level of quality is expected. So, in order to become repeatedly good at our business activities we first need to look at what is needed to create the standard of excellence and achieve success that repeats itself many times over. A good place to begin is to learn how leading companies achieve operational effectiveness, repeating success, and then benchmark our own individual operation.

High-maturity companies are different from their competitors in a way that is valuable to the consumer. They also have achieved operational effectiveness because they focus on six basic work processes. The best organizational structures create unity, teamwork, collaboration, and cooperation. This kind of structure is essential for implementing a unique strategy throughout the company. Low-maturity companies often lack a clearly defined position, an effective strategy and a dedicated commitment to basic work processes. Low-maturity companies are also undisciplined to adhere to these three things, typically having only sporadic and random success.

To avoid operating at a low-maturity level we must know to what extent to perform the six basic work processes activities. It is accomplished through activity integration, and is carried out by the company's leadership when they do strategic planning. This integration process helps managers know how to make their individual activities consistent with, and reinforcing of, the strategy.

Companies use hundreds of activities to design, develop, produce, sell, support, and deliver their goods or services to the consumer. These activities are categorized into two main groups, ***primary activities and support activities.*** All primary and support activities work reciprocally together in the terms of the value they create for the company and for the customer. The author uses Michael E. Porter's model describing how primary and support activities work together to form a value chain. The value chain model demonstrates a large scale grouping of activities but it does not define exactly the specific activities that each company performs. It serves as a guide to help a company know what activities it must embark on to create value. Each company needs to make a choice of what activities it will perform. Low-maturity business thinking leads to the addition of activities without too much consideration on how well they will fit within the strategy. The type of activities the company performs should be controlled by the company's strategy. This mandates that the company needs to choose what strategy it will pursue.

When a company's activities are said to be effective, it means that they support, reinforce and are optimized for the company's strategy—this is *operational effectiveness.* Strategy is the creation of a unique and valuable position within the market place by deliberately allocating company's resources to achieve sustainable competitive advantage.

Throughout this part the author employs a simple but relevant analogy with a building structure, where the six basic work processes create a strong foundation and the platform for launching initiatives represents the concrete slab poured above the foundation. These elements form operational effectiveness. Furthermore, the bearing walls of the building represent the strategy's points of differentiation and the roof is the strategy's theme, the tag line and the mission statement. The strategy is about being different in creating sustained competitive advantage. Companies can choose cost leadership strategy, differentiation strategy, or focus strategy but not more than one at a time; otherwise they will get caught in the middle, with disastrous effects. Any change in the value chain will have a direct positive or negative effect on the company's profit margins. Each link in the chain is inseparably connected to an integrated network of activities. The essence of strategy is to enhance the company's ability to earn and sustain healthy profits.

The journey to discover the "ins and outs" of management and leadership ends with an epilogue influenced by the thoughts and actions of one of the great contemporary leaders, Colin Powel, former U. S. Secretary of State. Powel urges to *"Fit no stereotypes. Don't chase the latest management fads. The situation dictates which approach best accomplishes the team's mission".* Effective management and leadership could be exercised over time and over a wide array of responsibilities; across an entire business organization involving a variety of people, accomplishing a multitude of tasks. The leadership must entice high performance and assure the well being of the whole group. Good managers and leaders focus relentlessly on making sure that their best performers are the most satisfied because ultimately it is people that make the difference between organizational success and failure.

Empowered working atmosphere is a beneficial factor in the advancement of managers to the goal of becoming great leaders. Good leaders are breaking the pattern, continuously reshaping the mold when the innovations thrive. They continuously root out the barriers of communication and the flow of information both inward and outward. They understand the importance of rejecting the superficial evaluation, and delve into the underlying reality. They continue to probe deeper in search for discerning the truth from smoke. The mediocre manager will basically carry out standing orders and passively wait for new ones to come down the chain of command. In contrast the best managers are constantly operating at the leading edge of their responsibility spectrum and sometimes they are leaning over the boundaries, beyond their job description; they often feel empowered enough as not to ask anyone's permission. They experiment, regularly trying out new methods with their teammates. They avoid complacency and think outside the box. They respect the box but constantly and tactfully challenge the status quo.

Nothing can thwart you, the aspiring or the seasoned manager from doing precisely that, also.

CHAPTER I

BUSINESS FUNDAMENTALS

"Good management consists in showing average people
how to do the work of superior people".
John D. Rockefeller

To understand management and leadership in today's business climate, first it needs to be understood what businesses or other types of socio-economical organizations are and how they operate (*1).

A business creates goods or provides a service to its customers. A manufacturer produces goods which in turn are sold to other businesses or to individuals through *wholesalers* who buy in large quantities, or through *retailers* who purchase goods from wholesalers and resell to individual customers, one or a few at a time. In return, the customers pay for the goods or services. The money received from the customer represents the business' revenue. A service business provides, as the name implies, a service to other businesses or to individuals.

To provide goods or services, any business has certain expenses and generally speaking the difference between the revenue and expenses constitutes the net income. If the net income is greater than zero then the business is creating a profit for the owners or shareholders and it is said that it operates "in the black". The profit is what keeps companies alive and in business. If their profit dips below zero it is "in the red" (a reference to common spreadsheets which represent negative numbers in red font) and the business is losing money.

Not all companies operate for a profit. Some not-for-profit (or non-profit) organizations do not give any income to the owners but instead use all the net income to improve the organization. Examples of non-profit organizations are schools, hospitals and community services entities. Government agencies also are non-profit organizations of a special category.

Businesses don't operate in a void, but rather coexist within a business environment having economic, legal, competitive, and cultural ramifications. The economic factors influence a business on what kind and how much of a quantity of goods or services consumers purchase. Laws and regulations impose the framework for the businesses' operational system and competition affects the type of goods or services a business produces, the price it charges for them, the location of its operations and its markets.

Businesses that are involved in the **production of goods** typically deal with the flow of materials from raw to final consumer product. These businesses can be one of the three main types:

a)   *Manufacturers*—produce the goods for sale to other businesses or to individual customers. These goods may be the final product (such as refrigerators or television sets) or they may be just components (such as hard drives or computer chips) that are used in the assembly and manufacture of other final products. The manufacturer can produce goods out of basic materials or by using components purchased from other manufacturers. If the manufacturer sells goods outside the country it is called an *exporter*.

b)   *Wholesalers or Distributors*—buy the goods from a manufacturer in large quantities and store them in warehouses. Subsequently, they sell smaller quantities to retailers. Sometimes the manufacturer is also a wholesaler in which case the manufacturer sells directly to retailers and thus eliminating the middle step.

c)   *Retailers*—purchase quantities of goods from the wholesaler or in some cases directly from the manufacturer, keep the goods at the store and resell them in small quantities to the consumer. If the retailer purchases the goods from a manufacturer outside the country, the retailer becomes an *importer.*

A **service business** is not directly involved in the three aspects described above but rather provides a service needed by other organizations or directly by the consumer, called *the customer*. Some businesses provide services related to the goods manufactured and sold (as is the repair or delivery sector), and these services can in some instances be provided by one of the three categories of businesses mentioned above, or by a totally different company.

In other cases businesses provide services unrelated to the consumer goods, such as facility services or building maintenance. This is the sector targeted by this text.

Non-profit organizations, as opposed to for profit companies, provide goods and services (in most cases) without the intention of turning a profit. Good examples of non-profit organizations are Goodwill Industries or churches and charitable organizations.

Government is a special type of not-for-profit service business. Government makes and upholds laws and regulations that affect individuals and businesses. It provides also some basic services such as police, fire and rescue. These services are paid for with taxpayer money and with fees charged for the service.

The Functions of a Business

A business has the following major functions:

❖ *Manufacturing*—which sometimes is called production, is the function that produces the goods for sale. In manufacturing business this function is extremely large and important. In other businesses, such as a service business this function is usually non-existent and it may be replaced by a related function sometimes called *Operations* which performs various tasks, depending of the service provided.

❖ *Accounting*—records and reports financial information about the business. All types of businesses require the accounting function, but the details vary according to the type of business the company is involved in.

❖ *Financial*—obtains money needed by the business and plans its usage. Money for a company comes primarily from the sale of the goods produced or the services provided. But it may come from investments made by the company and from banks or other lending institutions which loan money to the company. Once the money is obtained it can be used for the daily activities, or it can be invested for future use. The financial function plans for the volume of money needed, determines the optimum method to acquire it and decides how it should be spent. The financial function is closely related to the accounting function, but is separate, despite the tendency of a lot of businesses to create one department for both, called sometimes the accounting and finance department.

❖ *Human Resources Management*—in some cases it is
  called Personnel Department and is in charge with
  hiring, training, remunerating and terminating
  employees. This is another function that all businesses
  need to have; some businesses that employ a large
  number of personnel require that this function be
  extensive, for recruiting needs, for skills assessment,
  and for training and retention. For other businesses
  where many or all employees perform similar types of
  work the Human Resources Management may not
  need to be as large (for example in some retail businesses).

❖ *Marketing*—sells the goods or services and it needs to
  first determine what products (or services) to sell and at
  what price. After that it must embark in product promotion and finally it must make the actual sale. All
  businesses have some kind of marketing function but
  this varies, from a very large function (as in retail businesses) to a fair size as in service businesses (where new
  accounts need to be sold continuously to provide
  growth and to counteract loss of contracts due to normal operation), to a small size, as in manufacturing
  business where the product is sometimes sold to only
  one wholesaler.

❖ *Other Functions*—these functions may be performed in
  certain cases. One is the *Research and Development*
  function which is responsible for developing new products to be manufactured or for innovative ways to provide a service. Another is the *Information Services*
  function which is responsible for providing computer
  information systems support.

There are also other functions that can be identified in certain types of businesses; the two mentioned above though are

the more common functions and are increasingly present throughout the business spectrum.

Information is used by the management to assist with decision making. A *decision* is described as making a selection between various courses of action. Information reduces the uncertainty and the risk of the future action. As part of the Information Services function, **Information Systems** or IS provide the technology and methods which support the information requirements and the standard processing of a business. They make information readily available and control the flow of it, improving the efficiency of any information processing activity, enhancing productivity and individual effectiveness.

TYPICAL BUSINESS ORGANIZATION

<u>PRESIDENT (CEO)</u>

OPERATIONS AREA

- Vice President of Operations
  - o Receiving Department
  - o Shipping Department
  - o Inventory Control Department
  - o Purchasing Department

MARKETING AREA

- Vice President of Marketing
  - o Billing Department
  - o Advertising Department
  - o Sales Manager (SALES DEPARTMENT)
    - Sales Person
    - Sales Person

- Sales Person
- Work Group
  - ✓ Sales Person
  - ✓ Sales Person

FINANCE AND ACCOUNTING AREA

- Vice President of Finance
  - ○ Finance Department
- Vice President of Accounting
  - ○ Accounts Receivable Department
  - ○ Accounts Payable Department
  - ○ Payroll Department
  - ○ General Accounting Department

HUMAN RESOURCES & LEGAL AREA

- Vice President of Human Resources
  - ○ Training and Developing Department
- Vice President of Legal Affairs
  - ○ Legal Department
  - ○ Risk Management Department
    - Loss Prevention Manager
    - Occupational Safety Manager

The employees of an organization are often grouped by the general type of function they are to perform. Each functional area then is divided into *departments*, which have specific responsibilities within the general function.

The employees of a department are organized in *work-groups* to perform specific tasks. Each department is led by a *manager* who is in charge of all the people working within that department. All the department managers in a functional area report to a *functional area manager* who, in large organizations is often called *vice president*. Furthermore all these functional area managers or vice presidents report to the *general manager of the business* who is usually the *president* or the *chief executive officer*. Below is an example of an organizational chart for a wholesale business, although it may be applied to other types of businesses with minor modifications.

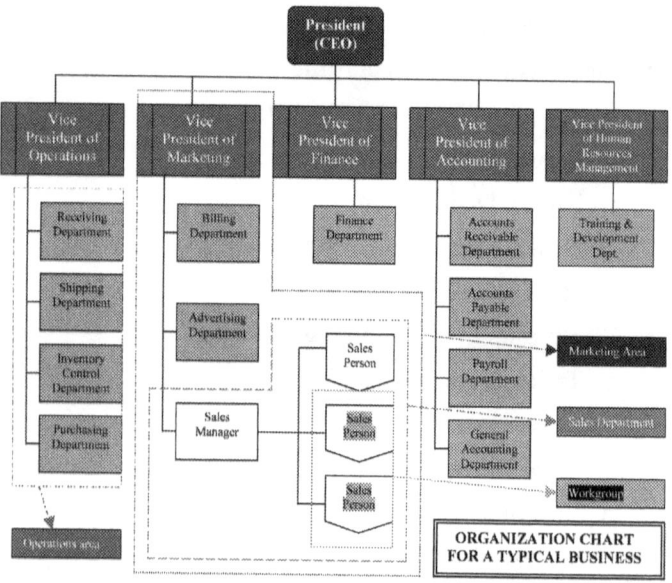

For example, in building services businesses the Operations Area under the Vice President of Operations will be replaced by regions, made up of districts, which are made up of areas or small accounts, or large stand-alone accounts.

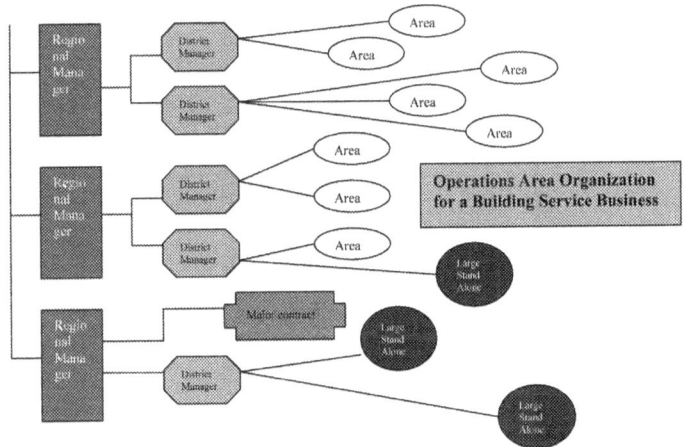

Operations Area Organization for a Building Service Business

The organizational structure of a company varies for different type of businesses. For example a manufacturer would replace the Operations Area with Production Area; others would combine the accounting and finance areas.

Yet others might have other functions such as Information Services and/or Research & Development Department(s).

In some cases businesses utilize structures which are not based on business functions. As an example, there are businesses which organize employees by geographic area or by product type.

CHAPTER II

INTRODUCTION TO MANAGEMENT

"Management is nothing more than motivating other people"
Lee Iacocca, Former CEO of Chrysler Corporation

Training is the quintessential factor in the long-term success of any company. The great leaders of contemporary economical and market-oriented societies strive to introduce innovative thinking and ideas in training methods to enable the wide range of management personnel to succeed.

As we delve into the challenging and more often than not very rewarding world of management, we need to first get an overall view of the models that will be used throughout this text, which will allow the achievement of excellence.

The first is **The Overall Quality Model,** which employs sound business practices and naturally drives quality inside any area or circumstance it is applied: family, business endeavor, school, non-profit organization, and so on.

It consists of five stages:

1) **Personal Development,** which is electing and applying core principles that govern individual life. It also contains a means of measuring the progress and

personal growth, along with level IV planning, which will be explained in detail later in the text.

2) **Interpersonal Skills Development**, which is creating win-win situations and paradigms, influencing other people, and at the same time making friends along the way. Developing personal industry knowledge and empathetic listening will go a long way towards mastering the art of management and leadership.

3) **Managerial Development** through empowerment at personal and team level. It calls for creating a team-work atmosphere by establishing a team mission statement and guidelines, team member functions and rewards. It nevertheless calls for focusing attention equally at the four areas of the aforementioned Equilibrium Square.

4) **Organizational Development**, which is aligning the job descriptions with the job expectations, and by leveling the performance evaluations across the board. Coaxing the corporate view with the strategic planning agreed upon by the Company's Board of Directors is another important aspect of organizational development leading to the differentiation between low-maturity and high-maturity organizations. Aligning the training program to the vision of the company allows organizational effectiveness. Aligning the intended processes with the technology that is available or is planned to be acquired entices operational efficiency.

5) **Level V Leadership.** Evolving to this level is defined by Jim Collings in his recent work "Good to Great" as building "enduring greatness through a paradoxical blend of personal humility and professional will".

The other model used in this book is the **Equilibrium Square**, intended to create habits to attribute equal importance to the main four areas of responsibility of a service business: *Customer Relations and Satisfaction, Operational Effectiveness, Financial Performance* and *Marketing*. By balancing the efforts in these areas any service business will achieve long-term growth and profitability.

1) **Customer Relations and Satisfaction** enhancement leads to an increase of business and customer retention, creates value-added services for the customer and breeds win-win situations. A satisfied customer will always improve a company's well being and reputation, enhancing at the same time the industry's image.

2) **Operational effectiveness** is achieved by implementing and observing all the aspects of the organization's Quality Assurance program. Technology usage, if aligned with the internal processes used by the organization can confer a *strategic impact* by providing a competitive advantage in the marketplace (*1).

3) **Financial performance** is what keeps all business afloat. It allows companies to improve their cash flow and achieve competitive profits by reducing costs and debt through healthy ratios.

4) **Marketing** is the new business generator and is what exposes the company and its services to the outside world, attracting new prospects and enhancing the image among the competitors. It allows vertical growth and directly contributes to an organization's overall growth and expansion.

These two models work symbiotically; one assists in leadership and the other in management; both with the unique purpose of providing a benchmark for achieving excellence.

In traditional quality control the main method used is inspection. The manager inspects (with the subconscious intention of finding defects), rates the findings and then contacts subordinates whose area of responsibility covers the inspected facility to point out the defects that need to be corrected. This method is inherently reactive—by the time the inspection takes place, it is already too late—the damage (or defect) already happened, exposing the manager to embarrassment (to say the least), frustration, and a tendency to over-react. It demands a lot of time and effort to correct the problem, increasing expenses, and creates a vicious cycle with minimal achievement.

Another problem with this paradigm is that it is based on an erroneous concept which assumes that quality control is achieved by employing drastic inspection methods, to the detriment of personal-driven quality that occurs naturally and is intrinsically founded on the principles of effectiveness and efficiency.

True quality involves more than a well written inspection process—it calls for a company's business culture, created in accordance with adherence to core principles. True quality demands that equal attention needs to be imparted to all the stages depicted below: personal, inter-personal, managerial and organizational.

Personal stage (**stage one**) deals with one's self. It recognizes the idea that an organization's capacity to create quality is directly proportional with the sum of all individual employees' ability to create quality. It is crucial that the principles of self-imposed quality be driven at each individual's level and each person needs to reach for quality in everything they do in their personal lives.

"We are what we repeatedly do. Excellence is not an act but a habit" is how Aristotle very concisely stated it.

High quality is a product of people whose daily activities are based upon natural laws and principles, such as hard work, discipline, honesty, integrity, etc. The trust in someone is achieved through adherence to the above principles. Therefore, if a pattern of adherence to these principles is observed in someone's conduct it can be a sure sign of achieving overall quality regardless of circumstances or obstacles.

If someone violates these principles then the opposite result is achieved, leading to failure.

The personal stage is totally necessary for the success and growth in the other stages. When it is accomplished, trust is born allowing relationships founded on trustworthiness to be further developed in the next stage.

Personal growth is not a product of chance; it is a deliberate choice, the result of continuous abiding to the natural principles of growth and the natural law of sacrifice. It means that someone needs to sacrifice time and effort to achieve growth.

Put in a mathematical form the *formula for growth* may look like this:

$$C_{haracter} = (P_{aradigms} + A_{ctions} + H_{abits}) * S_{acrifice}$$

Starting the calculation within the parentheses we need to label **paradigms**. They define the way everyone thinks and accordingly, they drive everyone's actions in a particular way. Our thoughts and perceptions of the surrounding environment, cultural factors and heritage create our paradigms.

If a person sets as a target to achieve maximum production with his team but his paradigm is that people are lazy, irresponsible, and need to be micro-controlled, that person will never achieve the set goal. The result will always be untrustworthiness, manipulation and double-mindedness.

But by employing a paradigm shift, along with the determination to follow the rest of the formula, the target can be eventually achieved.

Actions are determined by thoughts. *"I think, therefore I am!"* enunciates Aristotle in an age-old statement. We can pre-visualize the course of our actions which sometimes motivates us and sometimes discourages us, making us become what we think we are.

The next factor in the formula is **Habits**, as being a continuous relation between thinking and action (think-act-evaluate-think-act-evaluate, etc). Research demonstrated that if a thought-action relationship is sustained for 26 consecutive days, it forms a habit. This is a learned habit, and what is learned if is not effective can be un-learned with time and effort. It then can be replaced with a more effective learned habit. The research further demonstrate that learning and its counterpart, the un-learning, happen at the connection level of the brain. As we accumulate our portfolio of thoughts, emotions, feelings, and actions the connections made by our neurons that support this collection are fortified and create strong "communication access ways" for the neurons' activity. What we use regularly becomes stronger and stronger, creating long lasting effective habits. At the same time, the connections in the brain that are seldom used become diluted and eventually vanished. If there's a choice between two alternatives, the one containing a more elaborate and richer network of neurons will always win out, and the thicker, stronger the communication access way becomes. When the habits have been acquired through repetition learning and practice, the strong pathways developed become the "default" access way for the brain— therefore we act instantly, automatically and subconsciously. So, we can conclude that an accumulation of habits create competencies allowing us to get the work done well. Conversely, if a habit becomes dysfunctional, the act of replacing it with a more appropriate one requires long practice of blocking it so that a newly learned habit can take the void.

Multiplying the sum of our habits, actions, and paradigms by the sacrifice we are willing to make, creates our **character**.

"Character is doing good when no one's looking" is a slogan widely used on today's political scene to emphasize someone's great character. The more sacrifice (in time and effort), the stronger the character is.

So if we want to grow, we need to follow this formula of personal growth without faking it or trying shortcuts.

Interpersonal stage (stage two) incorporates the personal stage along with the skills in interpersonal and societal relationships. These skills need to be practiced and enhanced continuously in order to have excellence. A good example here is the way some apathetic government employees display their "interpersonal skills or lack thereof" when providing service, leading to frustration, disgust, and anger.

This stage is dependent upon achieving the previous stage, for it is impossible to appear genuine in interpersonal relations without reaching success on the personal stage. We may even come across as having a hidden agenda, being manipulative, or unsound. That is because without sound principles one does not care much for creating true and long-lasting relationships.

Skipping the personal stage and concentrating on the next one asks for trouble. It is an indication of someone's intent for a quick fix as a solution, because building good habits takes time. It is an easy-out road that returns the least amount of growth and requires the last amount of effort.

Nevertheless, if the interpersonal stage is based on the personal stage, the skills and actions of the interpersonal stage become effective means to express the principles we advocate.

The difference is sincerity. When trust is established, people tend to open up and allow to be influenced. Trust thus becomes the bonding compound that cements together the aggregates of great interpersonal relationships.

Managerial stage (stage three) is where the empowerment happens. Individuals successful and skilled in the previous two stages can be entrusted to make sound business decisions on their own, aligned with the organization's rules and regulations, without being held by the hand.

This stage bears indeed the fruits of achieving success in previous two stages. With trust earned in the first stage and trustworthiness formed in the second stage we are able to empower others so that they in turn can achieve the highest possible level of motivation and top performance. Thus, it stimulates and enhances involvement, responsibility and accountability.

The empowered management method is far superior. It is effective and satisfying because people manage themselves, providing better service to their customers and thus operating in a pro-active mode. They provide true quality at the end point of service where the impact on the customer is at its maximum, without waiting for approvals or for decisions to be made for them by the upper echelons in the hierarchy.

This management concept calls for embarking on the business endeavor the best prepared people first, put them in the best fit positions and disembark the ones that do not fit. With great people it is easy to reach great destinations.

Empowerment is a perfect fit for the homo-sapiens, being the expression of free enterprise based on a set of principles, rather than policies. It is the right medium for fostering innovation and is the catalyst for commitment and loyalty, providing the motivation behind overall quality. It fulfills some of the core human needs such as making people feel important in their activities, acknowledging and rewarding success or creating a sense of purpose and belongingness.

This book will assist in forming an overall quality paradigm through empowerment.

The **Organizational stage (stage four)** deals with the alignment of the company's organizational components and provides combustion for all the other stages by growing and supporting an overall quality corporate culture. It creates the possibility of enlightening the organization's leadership in recognizing the power of the previous three stages.

The components of the organizational stage are:

- ❖ A culture of discipline
- ❖ The Executive Council
- ❖ Company's expectations aligned with corresponding job descriptions
- ❖ Uniformity in company's performance evaluation, rewards and advancement norms
- ❖ Compensation plan aligned with industry's standards
- ❖ Hiring and development practices
- ❖ Use of modern technology to correlate with the processes in place

This stage is essential to the Overall Quality Model. In this stage the above components are synchronized to support and reinforce the previous three stages. If these components do not work in unison, they will undermine the very principles this model is based upon and creates a dysfunctional entity.

Let's analyze these components for a moment:

- ❖ Adhering to a culture of discipline. Jim Collings in his recent work "Good to Great" affirms that "All companies have a culture, some companies have discipline but few companies have a *culture of discipline.* When you have disciplined people you don't need hierarchy. When you have disciplined thought you don't need bureaucracy. When you have disciplined action you don't need excessive controls." By combining this culture with ethical entrepreneurship you get great performance. (*3)

❖ Alignment of the Executive Council to the model means that top management brass buys into the model to the extent that they walk, talk and breathe the model. The executives need to use core principles of making themselves and their subordinates accountable; they need to make it important to follow and monitor the progress of their management staff. It means that they create actions and opportunities that support the model, sacrificing self-interest for the greater good.

❖ Job descriptions aligned with the expectations means that individual responsibility is assigned, which fosters personal and interpersonal improvement and creates expectations or goals. It becomes a basic job duty by assigning the task of creating an empowered team environment.

❖ Uniformity in company's performance evaluation, rewards and advancement norms means that the personal improvement described above becomes the uniform basis for monetary compensation and advancement rather than tenure. These norms being aligned with the model make the performance along the model matter. It creates follow-up, commitment and accountability to the program. Alignment in advancement and rewards reinforces the importance of accountability and commitment to the overall quality model.

❖ Compensation plan aligned with industry's standards. Alignment in this component rewards an overall quality culture rather than merely creating a profit in order to stay afloat.

❖ Alignment in hiring and development practices provides on one hand a means of matching new hires to the company's overall quality model by targeting only the types of people that fit the model. On the other hand it provides the "selected few" new employees as well as the other seasoned ones with the means of getting sharper or staying sharp at what they do, building support to each other area of the model.

❖ Alignment in the use of modern technology to correlate with the processes in place helps facilitate the use of information, enhances communication, follow-up and feedback, ever so important in a service oriented business. The danger is that some companies try to use technology to create the quantum leap forward in quality. Great companies never use the technology primordially to fire up a transformation in quality but rather they are the pioneers in the implementation of very thoroughly and attentively selected technologies that best fit the model.

These four stages along with core principles form the foundation from where true quality evolves, leading to the highest stage: Level V.

At this **Level V Leadership (fifth stage)**, the intention is to create a complete paradigm that can evolve; one that can self-perpetuate overall quality culture throughout an organization. According to Jim Collings, "*Level V leaders channel their ego needs away from themselves and into the larger goal of building a great company.(...) Their (personal) ambition is first and foremost for the institution, not themselves*".(*3)

At the heart of these five stages are the governing forces called core principles or natural laws.

As an eloquent example, Benjamin Franklin worked throughout his life on what he called "moral perfection", creating his well-known "13 virtues":

- ❖ Temperance: Eat not to dullness; drink not to elevation.

- ❖ Silence: Speak not but what may benefit others or yourself; avoid trifling conversation.

- ❖ Order: Let all your things have their places; let each part of your business have its time.

- ❖ Resolution: Resolve to perform what you ought; perform without fail what you resolve.

- ❖ Frugality: Make no expense but to do good to others or yourself; i.e., waste nothing.

- ❖ Industry: Lose no time; be always employed in something useful; cut off all unnecessary actions.

- ❖ Sincerity: Use no hurtful deceit; think innocently and justly, and, if you speak, speak accordingly.

- ❖ Justice: Wrong none by doing injuries, or omitting the benefits that are your duty.

- ❖ Moderation: Avoid extremes; forbear resenting injuries so much as you think they deserve.

- ❖ Cleanliness: Tolerate no uncleanliness in body, cloths, or habitation.

- ❖ Tranquility: Be not disturbed at trifles, or at accidents common or unavoidable.

- ❖ Chastity: Rarely use venery but for health or offspring, never to dullness, weakness, or the injury of your own or another's peace or reputation.

- ❖ Humility: Imitate Jesus and Socrates.

"Franklin placed each one of these virtues on a separate page in a small book that he kept with him for most of his life. He would evaluate his performance with regard to each of them on a daily basis. He would also select one of the virtues to focus on for a full week" (*2).

Overall quality germinates from an organization that is built on enduring core principles. These principles are fundamental truths that were proven throughout human history and withstand time and transcend forms of government, philosophy, politics, science or religion. They constitute the bricks for building long-lasting and enduring success and rigorous and continuous adherence to them guarantees the outcome of the desired results.

MANAGER'S EFFECTIVENESS

What does it mean to be effective? As an individual, as a manager or as a company we want to be effective. We want to become a model or reference in our field and this can't be achieved by just doing an OK job, barely bumping along. We can't create excellence out of mediocrity. Creating excellence is possible only by becoming highly effective people in whatever we do. Highly effective people are those who enhance their pro-active skills, those who plan and organize instead of reacting and hiding from the truth. They are people who not only produce at high levels but also take care of the things that allow them to produce consistently at those high levels.

A manager acts in one or more of the four zones:

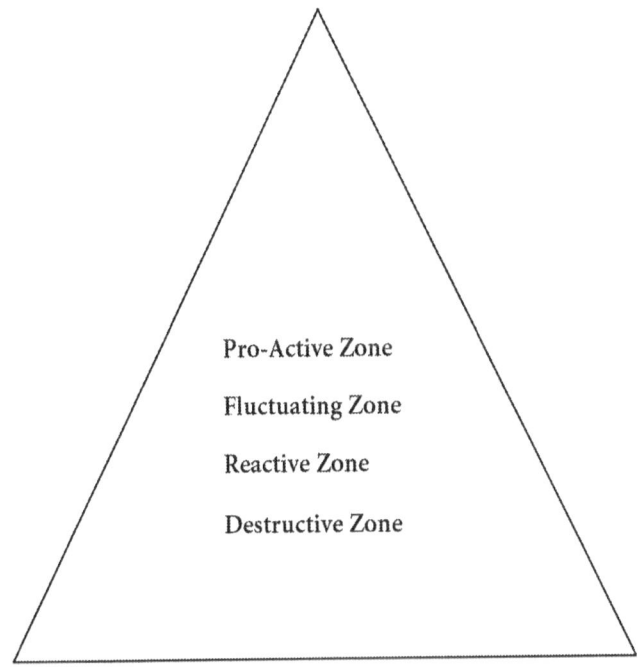

Pro-Active Zone

Fluctuating Zone

Reactive Zone

Destructive Zone

These zones create a *self-mastery triangle* where each one acts upon the zone(s) underneath.

Proactive Zone

It acts upon the other zones. People who managed to achieve proactive stage through self-mastering the triangle are those who act. They are positioned at the top because they lead the way. Their zone is pointing upward symbolizing their continuous improvement and progression. In a proactive stage people realize that it is not their poor circumstances, conditions or bad luck that affects them but rather the way they respond to these conditions or circumstances. I intentionally not used the work "react" to suggest that their actions are a lot more than just reacting. They are not affected by the other people's moods or the weather. When aversion is encountered they use words like:

- ❖ I will overcome
- ❖ I will control myself
- ❖ I will adapt
- ❖ I will choose
- ❖ I will be responsible for

From the onset of their thoughts, to their words and to their actions, these proactive people are in the driver's seat. A proactive stage helps them retain responsibility for their actions and for their response to external or internal stimuli. They retain the power to overcome the most difficult situations.

When we subsist in this proactive zone, we learn to influence our environment and the surrounding conditions rather than be influenced. We are conscientious of the fact that through our powers of self-evaluation, creativity and self-will we are able to adapt to any circumstance, we can overcome any obstacle and improve upon any situation.

So what does it mean to be an effective manager?

Most companies measure effectiveness according to criteria such as bottom line profit, quality scores, customer satisfaction, or sales and for the most part these measurements are correct. The effectiveness is measured to a certain extent by how much we produce. However, true effectiveness is based not only on producing, but rather on ensuring that the things which enable us to produce *keep continuing to produce.*

It comes down to good old-fashion self-mastery. For example, it is the easy way out to hire the first job applicant available and throw him into a job, filling an immediate need. In a proactive state of mind we need to look beyond just filling the position and hoping for performance; we need to be persistent in filling *each* position with *the right* person *all the time.*

Activities that take place in the proactive zone free individuals from things that bog them down or control them. A much appreciated former mentor used to say: *"Don't let the business run you, you run the business!"*

If we just wait for things to happen and then try to put out fires, we're doomed to failure. For instance, planning is one of the activities of the proactive zone. By planning we prepare ourselves for a future event which can eliminate the costly unknowns or even mistakes that occur frequently if we act haphazardly. A call or visit to a job site to make sure a subcontractor or a crew showed up for work eliminates an unpleasant email from a frustrated customer.

Proactive managers have a list of priorities aligned with their company's model, and they know how to refuse tasks which conflict with their priorities. The great English philosopher John Stuart Mill described a person in a possible proactive zone:*" He who lets the world or his portion of it, choose his plan of life for him has no need of any other faculty than the ape-like one of imitation. He who chooses his plan for himself employs all his faculties. He must use observation to see, reasoning and judgment to foresee, and activity to gather materials for decision (…) firmness and self-control to hold to his deliberate decision…"* (*4).

Fluctuating Zone

Most managers subsist in a fluctuating zone. They allow themselves to get caught up in the stress and time-consuming mode of the reactive zone, but frequently pull themselves out through proactive actions.

Everyone dips in the fluctuating zone at some point, for there is not a distinctive demarcation line between the two, but rather a "*zone of transition*". In this zone of transition we either progress towards pro-activity through self-mastery and discipline, or we take the easy way out and immerse into the reactivity.

Reactive Zone

This zone is towards the bottom of the triangle and rightfully so: it is a place of being acted upon. The reactive zone is a stressful and frustrating experience; it is floating aimlessly in deep water with no sight of land. In its upper levels, or in its *zone of transition,* most managers become **crisis managers**, putting out fires. They work hard but spend all their time treading water. They stay afloat but they remain adrift, not being able to go anywhere. Without any initiative, and thus elevating themselves into the fluctuating or even proactive stage, they tire and sink even deeper in reactivity, reaching its abyss called the destructive zone.

Destructive Zone

In this zone we feel as if our actions or behaviors are controlled by something else and we may be enticed to give up saying that "it is the nature of our industry, it comes with the territory".

Why most people subsist in the reactive or destructive zone? For they choose to take the path of least resistance. On a superficial analysis it may look as being the easiest road. Taking this easy road assures a lot of aimless hard work. It may be deceiving, even attractive at first because often people are praised for working long hours. But, there is a great fallacy. This reactive stage causes us to self-fulfill the very problem which we blame on other conditions. The harder and longer we work the worst the results seem to be. It becomes a vicious cycle of the status-quo: "I can't do anything about the situation, so it'll stay the same (or get worse)". As we abdicate responsibility of acting by forfeiting our creativity and determination to some other condition, we become powerless to change the circumstance. We can't often see that we have the power to choose, by being too busy treading water just to stay alive. This turns off our powers of self-evaluation, creativity and determination, sacrificing our abilities to the oppressing circumstance.

The secret of being highly effective is realizing that we have the power to choose our response to the condition that affects us. When there's something that has to be done and we don't feel like doing, but we do it nevertheless—we have the power to override the feelings or our moods for the greater good. When people move into a proactive state of mind and are willing to do the things that they don't feel like doing just for the sake of integrity, they are on their way to achieve a greater success.

The three human attributes that anyone can use to escape from the tyranny of the reactive stage are determination, creativity, and self-conscience.

Everyone has the power to change and the ability to evolve from reactivity to a proactive stage, whether they deal with ineffective behaviors, low profitability, or high turnover. Everyone has the ability to self-evaluate in identifying ineffective behaviors, or to use creativity for creating processes to counteract low productivity or high turnover. It just takes discipline and the willingness to learn how to incorporate the abilities to evaluate, create, and then follow through.

How do we know in which stage we're operating? The answer may give us a clear picture of what to do to move from a reactive stage to a superior one.

All our activities can be divided in four categories (*35):

A. *Important but not urgent.* These activities reduce circumstances that control us. Some of these activities are:

❖ Planning and Organizing

- ❖ Creating balance
- ❖ Empowering activities
- ❖ Building relationships
- ❖ Directing and overseeing
- ❖ Fulfilling other's needs
- ❖ Training and/or self-improvement
- ❖ Performance evaluation and feedback; self-evaluation
- ❖ Measurement, follow-up and public relations
- ❖ Supporting and encouraging others
- ❖ Preventive maintenance
- ❖ Recreation/hobbies

B. *Not important but urgent.* These are annoying activities that act upon us and waste our time. Examples of these activities are:

- ❖ Focusing on methods rather than results
- ❖ Interruptions (phone calls, walk-ins, etc.)
- ❖ Popular activities (like "bring-your-child-to-work day")
- ❖ Pressing matters that focus on mistakes rather than on methods of eliminating them
- ❖ Some endless or pointless meetings

C. *Important and urgent.* These things act upon us and control us. Examples:

- ❖ Crisis situations
- ❖ Customer complaints
- ❖ Labor shortages or disputes
- ❖ Supplies shortages

❖ Breakdowns

❖ Payroll

❖ Special requests

❖ Phone calls, pages, emails

D. *Not important and not urgent.* These activities are a waste of time and render us unproductive:

❖ Gossip, complaining, criticizing

❖ Busy work, jumping from an activity to another

❖ Excessive worrying

❖ Watching TV

❖ Surfing the Internet

Using the Self-Mastery Triangle analogy, the top zone incorporates activities in category A; the next zone incorporates category B, and so forth.

Activities in category "A" form the proactive zone and work akin to antibodies; they attack irregular entrant particles, keeping our bodies in control and in good health. These "antibody" activities combat and eliminate most, if not all, of the non-productive and destructive activities which cause problems or waste our time. Therein lays the "secret of effectiveness": *effective managers are those who act within the proactive zone.* There's hope in the concept that if we can learn how to continuously act within the proactive zone we can eliminate the stress of the reactive zone or the self-annihilation inherent with the destructive zone.

Activities in category "B" are part of the fluctuating zone and represent the "not important" category. It is here that most people get stuck, because even if these activities are deemed not important they're urgent and they steal our time away from completing proactive activities. The more we reduce proactive activities the greater the risk of falling into reactivity and lose sight of really important activities.

Many people succumb to the interruptions by altering their course of action when these interruptions occur. Others spend endless hours in pointless meetings, just to satisfy their ego, without really accomplishing anything.

When working in this fluctuating zone we often believe that we're carrying on activities that are not only urgent but also important, whereas the truth is that they are not important. Acting in this zone creates only short term results fostering crisis management and shallow relationships. We feel victimized at times and perceive our goals as worthless and our plans as without merit.

Reactive activities, in category "C" deemed important and urgent, occur when operating in the reactive zone. This zone constitutes a huge trap because often people while acting in this zone are erroneously perceived as workaholics. It can be addictive and one may even enjoy the praise of working hard and being so committed. This work style leaves little time for anything else because of the huge undertaking required to constantly putting out fires. Working hard doesn't automatically mean working effectively.

In the reactive zone most of the proactive activities such as planning or goal setting are perceived as annoying interruptions in getting the work done. "I've been doing this for so many years, I know what to do; I don't have time to set goals" is a comment often heard among reactive managers when challenged with planning activities.

Although proactive activities represent tools for making us more effective, while operating in the reactive zone it is hard to delegate or to build others, because we get used to do things ourselves. The ages-old adage that if you want a thing done right you do it yourself does not work in effective management. In the reactive zone we rob ourselves of resources like empowerment, delegation, and training because it seems that there's no time for any of that. It brings so much stress that we can call it "*The Burnout Zone*". Even though many people survive all their life in the reactive zone, they escape into the destructive zone as momentary relief to justify their un-enviable situation.

The destructive zone incorporates the lowest of the activities in the reactive zone, some of which are depicted in category "D". Here we become self-destructive, useless or both, having a hard time holding a job. Some of the results of this zone are job loss, dependence on others, irresponsibility and being on defensive at all times.

Don't be fooled though, it's so easy to slip in this zone! We can be highly proactive in some areas and destructive in others if we engage in "water cooler folklore", gossip about coworkers, rumors about the company trends, or spend our time criticizing and complaining. If we're looking forward to improving our proactive skills, the only way this can be achieved is by eliminating the time and effort spent in the reactive *and* the destructive zones altogether.

We ought to take a breather and evaluate where we are at this point in time, by looking at the majority of our activities that make up our day. This way we can figure out in which zone we operate. We'll find ourselves probably in more than one. Knowing where we are and what path to take to achieve greatness in a good start. For that we also need a strategic plan.

THE STRATEGIC PLAN IN MANAGEMENT

All companies that plan to be around a long time have a strategic plan. Understanding this strategic planning helps aspiring managers in setting their own short term goals in order to achieve the company's long term targets. Also, it helps identifying opportunities. These opportunities can be located by analyzing an organization's *value chain*, which is defined as being an array of activities that add value to the finite product created by the said organization. If some activities in the value chain can be finalized in such a manner as to providing value-added to a product, then the business temporarily obtains a competitive advantage, until the competition catches up. Savvy managers can set their short term goals to fall within this area creating a competitive advantage and making themselves more valuable to their organization.

A strategic plan for a for-profit organization has four areas of responsibility, outlining The Equilibrium Square: **Customer Relations and Satisfaction**, **Operational**, **Financial Performance** and **Marketing**.

Management's focus should be to act equally on all four areas of responsibility thru planning, organizing, directing and controlling, rather than acting on only one or two areas. Why is that? Because by switching back and forth between these areas to put out fires is stressful at best. Keeping a balance (equilibrium) among these four business aspects yields serenity and the likelihood of success. For example, a manager empowers her employees to foster an atmosphere of overall quality, increases customer satisfaction, performs adequately in the financial area of responsibility and keeps a fresh stream of new accounts coming in. Then, the manager's rewards are less turnover, less complaints and greater volume, which leads to recognition, praise, personal satisfaction, and so on.

The Equilibrium Square concept allows managers to impart equal attention and an equal degree of importance to all four areas of responsibility by achieving and maintaining the following objectives:

Customer Satisfaction Objectives:
* create win-win partnerships
* create value-added services

❖ to be perceived by the customer as the standard of excellence

Operational Effectiveness Objectives:

❖ create full quality management all throughout the company by using the Overall Quality Model

❖ increase training and learning of the service industry's principles and the Overall Quality Model norms by developing team members

❖ empower team members

❖ provide the access to technology at all necessary levels that increase productivity and service quality

❖ cultivate and promote company's culture of discipline

Financial Performance Objectives:

❖ reduce operational costs

❖ make a minimum of 7% profit. Studies show that if a company creates less than 5% profit it will not stay afloat and if it generates more than 12% profit it attracts new competition making it harder to achieve the targeted profit margin.

Marketing Objectives:

❖ increase exposure in the targeted markets

❖ create turbo growth by maximizing opportunities

❖ build a vision, dream a little, and have fun while at it

It's all about equilibrium and continuous stability. To add more accountability and attention to the financial performance alone, leads to the deterioration of the other three areas of responsibility. We may achieve an impressive bottom line, but how long will that last if the customers become dissatisfied, the employees disgruntled and there's a lack of new business coming in? It doesn't matter which areas of responsibility we focus more on, if we don't act balanced by increasing all four equally, we put ourselves between a rock and a hard place.

Focusing on all four areas of responsibility brings value to both the company and its team members. For example, in achieving the operational effectiveness objectives the company makes an investment for developing its teams. From here, the team members enhance their abilities and thus the chances to move up in the company's chain of leadership. At the same time the company increases its performance and its competitiveness in the industry.

Customer Satisfaction Objectives

1.   Partnerships

A partnership is created when the company's human core and the customer work together with the commitment to honestly improve relationships and performances in order to make the business flourish and long lasting. In a partnership each party agrees to recognize one another's issues and subsequently work together without any hidden agendas to solve these issues. It is the key to a successful partnership. When both entities have this attitude creating partnerships overcome the obstacles which, more often than not, impede productivity and efficiency. This translates into competitive business for both parties. Creating partnerships with the customer significantly reduces the stress associated with problem-solving, because the customer is willing to work out the problems with you, giving you feedback and often contributing to the solution. Partnerships won't excuse underperformance, but when an honest effort for continuous improvement exists, it creates successful partnerships.

Without partnering with your client, you are dismissed before having a shot at solving the impeding problem.

2. Value-Added Service

A major component to a successful partnership is the value-added service. A strategic objective should be to maximize value-added services to all of the company's customers *within the company's financial capability.* Value-added services are those services exceeding the contractual specifications, benefiting the customer beyond the contracted work. One example is that a customer is relieved of some of the administrative duties inherent to outsourcing if the hired contractor provides a central dispatch system such as a Customer Service Center, which is interconnected with and provides feedback to the customer.

These value-added services can be performed without "giving away the farm" if the cost of operation is reduced by increasing efficiency. By accomplishing a task quicker you have time to accomplish a duty that is not part of the regular scope of work but it may be a hot button for your customer.

Also value-added service is personalized service. It comes not only from the management but it needs to be determined and to come from the front line team members as well.

3. Perceived as Standard of Excellence

The only way this perception can be created is through the interaction the customer has with the company representatives. The customer will judge the entire company by the quality of service they receive.

Operational Effectiveness Objectives

This is arguably one of the most misunderstood and neglected area in the services industry and at the same time is crucial to success. How effective a company is in executing its processes and procedures determines how well it measures up to the image it tries to convey to the customer. The target is to create an over-all quality environment which is structured on empowering all the team members directly proportionate with their position. This way, they get the opportunity to make sound decisions; they have a chance to act responsively and responsibly. It fulfills a basic human need—the need to feel important. Empowerment atmosphere creates as a result a stable and progressive environment.

True effectiveness is not determined entirely on the volume produced. It is rather determined by the ability to maintain and care for the elements which contribute to the activity of producing; the elements that keep the ball rolling. Anyone can make a short-lived profit to the detriment of quality of service or to the expense of the team members. The idea is to create true effectiveness while maintaining an even keel.

1.   Overall Quality Management

Continuous improvement in quality should be a company's main goal. The company needs to adopt the Overall Quality Model style. It is nothing amazingly new, for this concept is used to some degree in all industries. Overall Quality Model concept will be expanded later in this text. However, some quick basics about it are:

- ❖ employee empowerment
- ❖ prevention
- ❖ zero defects
- ❖ continuous improvement
- ❖ constant use of metrics and measurements
- ❖ forward and long term thinking

This text intends to help managers increase their capabilities in using Overall Quality Model principles. By adopting and implementing an Overall Quality Model vision during training and then using Overall Quality Model daily in your operation you can create long-term job stability and increase personal value.

2. Develop Team Members

This is essential for effectiveness. It is why employees are required to be certified in their positions. The dedication to development eliminates the trial and error method that is costly and rather unproductive. Furthermore team development enhances the principles of Overall Quality Model which call for prevention and zero defects. This text will assist managers in creating the skills and knowledge needed to select and recruit quality people that are right for the job at hand.

3. Empower Team Members

Empowerment is a key ingredient in effectiveness. It means getting everyone in the organization involved in the quality process and allowing them to make key decisions *within the framework of their organization's highly developed system,* for the success of their specialty. This does not mean that everyone is encouraged to make *any* decision on-the-fly that fits the occasion; it requires to make *the best-suited decision aligned and within the parameters of responsibility and job description,* with some degree of flexibility that is forethought and clearly explained to all team members ahead of time.

Empowerment involves enlarging and enhancing job descriptions. As the empowerment increases, the level of supervision should (and will) decrease because, generally speaking, people become more dependable and their capability of making sound business judgment increases as their level of accountability and responsibility raises.

Empowerment disseminates a sentiment of self-achievement among team members and encourages personal enhancement.

The principle of empowerment requires quality personnel and induces us to take great care in selecting and hiring the right people who can work independently and are self-motivated. Hiring only the people that fit the model and who can contribute beyond their job description mandated skills helps build an involved team that will satisfy the company's short-term objectives as well as its long-term strategy.

4.   Provide Access to Technology

For management personnel the use of technology and information systems assists in decision making effectiveness by providing related up-to-date and pertinent information for the decision at hand. They reduce the risk factor involved in decision-making and the outcome can be forecasted with an acceptable degree of accuracy. Management needs accurate and current information for *operational* and marketing decisions, to make *tactical* and *strategic* decisions and a *management information system* (MIS) brings all these to the manager's fingertips. MIS provides reporting capabilities and query functions to meet management requirements at any level of a business. It maintains one or several databases and the transaction processing systems' stored data is the main input for the MIS.

Access to the newest technology available in the service industry also enhances personal productivity, defined as how much and how fast an employee contributes to a business. It confers a *strategic impact* by providing a competitive advantage in the marketplace. Reducing the operational costs (cost leadership), identifying market niches (creating opportunity) or providing product differentiation (enhancing company's image within the industry) are only a few advantages of using and accessing the *right* technology.

5.   The Culture of Discipline

Creating a culture of discipline starts with *disciplined people*. It is not achieved by trying to discipline the wrong people into the right behaviors but by recruiting self-disciplined ones to begin with. Next is *disciplined thought* to stay the course. Finally it takes *disciplined action*. (*3)

This culture should not be mistaken as being a tyrannical cult of discipline, but rather as self-imposed. It needs to be constructed with responsibility and freedom of decision making within the aforementioned framework *and* it needs to be augmented with disciplined people.

Financial Performance Objectives

1.   Reduce Operational Costs.

"A penny saved is a penny earned" is an old adage that applies very well here. Managers are hired in their positions to be of value and to produce or to save company money. By using the training opportunities and with the use of technology managers are employed primarily to be efficient and effective, thus creating processes that contribute to the reduction of the cost of operations *without affecting overall quality*. Reducing this cost also saves customers' money implicitly, fostering customer satisfaction and enduring partnerships.

2.   Creating a Profit.

This is what keeps a business alive. The profit should be spread over four areas: rewarding the customer, rewarding the team members, rewarding the owners or shareholders and finally funding the investments that allow the company to achieve the standard of excellence or to be the best at what it does (being number two sometimes may not be good enough because in some management circles being number two is perceived as being the first loser).

A service oriented company needs to expend a great deal of financial resources to provide their customers with the best quality. Nothing less is acceptable. This means **rewarding the customer.** By investing in quality team members, good training and top of the line equipment the company is able to create great customer service.

How does rewarding the customer benefit you as a company employee? It cements a lasting partnership by helping your customer win and be appreciated. It makes the customer look good. The result is that your customer acts as your partner, being more tolerable when problems arise. There's nothing greater than having customers working to solve your problems as you work to solve theirs.

Just as a company works to reward its customers, it also **rewards its team members and its owners or shareholders.** A successful company shares profits with employees and owners through year-end performance bonuses, profit sharing, incentive programs, fringe benefits and investments in personal training and development. It rewards the shareholders by offering a greater return on investment. If the company takes care of its team, the team members will take care of the company.

Marketing Objectives

1.   Increase Exposure in the Targeted Markets.

A targeted market for a service oriented company could be for example large high tech accounts, large stand-alone buildings or bundled contracts. A marketing strategy is thus designed to maximize the overall available resources. Large high tech and large stand alone buildings create greater exposure and confer the opportunity of referrals and repeat business. They offer greater volume and thus operational flexibility without creating logistical problems. By following the marketing plan the result is an increase in available resources, greater volume and a concrete opportunity in receiving an enhanced paycheck without major time increase. The right marketing strategy is the best way to improve success in all of the other three areas of responsibility which form the Equilibrium Square.

2.   Create Turbo Growth.

This objective calls for creating the critical functions for growth: Planning. It means identifying targets and setting goals. It means creating benchmarks against which marketing performance is measures. It means creating a strategic business plan at each threshold along the way. It means preparing resources. In order to bring value, we need to enhance our resources and to build our people; we need to apply the principles. This will lead to accelerated (turbo) growth.

3.   Create Vision/Mission for lasting confidence.

Know where we are going in life. Creating a vision and a mission of what we want out of life will provide us with some direction and momentum to move forward. People who are low in confidence and those that are generally stuck in a rut lack some direction and purpose to their life and therefore just drift along, letting events happen to them rather than going out and making them happen. When we have a compelling vision, we will feel good about ourselves. We know where we are going in life and have a purpose to it all. A true mission has to express our purpose for existence.

CHAPTER III

MANAGEMENT ONE-ON-ONE

"The best executive is the one who has sense enough to pick good men to do what he wants done. And self-restraint to keep from meddling with them while they do it."
Theodore Roosevelt, 26th US president, 1901-1909

Key ingredients to management

Along with the responsibilities implied by accepting any job there are some fundamental components to all management positions. They will determine the attitude of advancement in management career and the altitude of success.

The purpose of management is to:

❖ Plan

❖ Organize

❖ Direct and

❖ Control

This purpose is illustrated on the next page. Let's take a closer look at these four aspects of management.

Plan

As a manager you are expected to be a planner. "Failure to prepare is preparing to fail" it's been said over and over through the years. Planning is preparing. Said Norman Vincent Peale: *"Plan your work for today and every day, then work your plan"* (*5).

By failing to plan, circumstances arise that begin to control you. Consider this example: You fail to plan for the quantity of supplies necessary for the month. You also fail to plan for the adequate delivery scenario.

Half way through the month, you receive a call that at the *site x* they are out of a key item. You need to rush to the warehouse, pick up the necessary item and deliver it to the site. In the mean time another *site y* across town calls to report a shortage on another important item. You rush back to the warehouse, pick up a speeding ticket along the way, grab the necessary supplies and head to the location. By the time you get there the shift is over, the workers are gone and you face a dilemma: should you finish the job yourself now, on your own time or call your customer, tail between your legs and apologize for your own lack of planning, hoping that you'll have a job the next day.

You start working deep into the Reactive Zone, losing control.

Planning allows you to work all these kinks out so that you remain in control of your actions. Failing to do so you'll abdicate to the demands coming out of every variable and you'll be acting like a leaf blowing in whichever direction the wind blows. Managers need to plan daily, weekly, monthly and annually. If you catch yourself saying that you don't have time to plan is because you failed to plan in the first place.

Set objectives and state the mission.

There are three crucial questions you must ask to obtain a clear objective: "*What* are you doing?", "*Why* are you doing it?" and "*Which* is the result of doing it?"

You need to ask these three questions every time you plan. If not, work becomes aimless, similar with driving in an unfamiliar town without a road map or any directions. It is very unlikely that someone will arrive at the right destination and in time in this manner. The same stands true for someone who doesn't plan. They may look busy but the fact is that it is very difficult to arrive at their destination without defining the location they're at, the destination they want to reach, the purpose for getting there and the direction to take.

Failing to state the objective and the mission is why many managers are wasting valuable time spinning their wheels. They seem busy but they are not really accomplishing anything. They may be making a profit but they are not increasing it. They may be OK for their jobs but they are not doing anything to move up in their jobs. This is the perfect description of acting in the Reactive Zone. To the contrary, establishing a clear objective and direction is essential in good planning.

Examine Options and Determine Resources

Once you know where to go and how to get there, good planning involves examining your options. By asking the question "What are the different ways to get where I'm going and what resources will help me getting there?" If you were driving to your intended destination you would probably use a road map. You would probably also be listening to a local radio station for a traffic report. The road map would show you the direct line to get to the destination and based on the traffic report you can determine alternative ways to get there.

Once you know how you are to get to your destination you must determine what the best resources are. Say you want to eliminate defects in workmanship. You may define this as "Using Overall Quality Model as a Guideline". Then you may list as your resources an experienced colleague who can share his/her experience with you, or use your training department for guidance.

Whatever you do, determining the best way to "get there" and the best resources available along the way can save you a lot of time and grief in the long run by preventing activities that are incompatible with your plan.

Create strategies

To accomplish any plan with effectiveness, you must have viable strategies that will help your work. This may mean creating new processes, changing your paradigm, influence people, changing behaviors and so on. Inevitably your plan will deal with people at some point so you have to use strategies that fit well with human performance. These strategies must be geared towards meeting the needs of those people involved in your plan. To do this you must understand human needs and how to use them. These needs will be explained later in this text.

Create timeline

If you don't set a timeline for your plan, it will be missing the needed accountability edge that helps drive and motivate yourself in the follow through process. In essence the plan is doomed to fail simply because you failed to work it. To make the timeline viable, keep it simple, realistic and make it visually appealing. By doing so, you will be more inclined to review your timeline frequently.

Planning can involve diverse amounts of time in the future, which are called "*planning horizons*" (*1). There are basically three types of planning and scores of savvy managers from sophisticated and highly successful Fortune 500 companies engaged in them. They are:

- ❖ Operational Planning
- ❖ Tactical Planning
- ❖ Strategic Planning

<u>Operational Planning</u>

Operational planning is the skill of employing our daily, weekly and monthly means to help us function properly. That is why it is sometimes also called "*functional planning*". Functional planning has a planning horizon of a few days to a few weeks, stretching to as long as a few months. For example working on the next week's work plan or penciling a Gantt chart to make sure you finish your next project before the end of the month so that you can post your revenue on this month's P&L represent operational or functional (immediate) planning. This means we take time to see exactly *what* needs to be done, the *best way* to do it and the *order of priority* it should be done in. Whatever it is work, family or civic duties operational planning helps us to stay focused and to work effectively.

Because of the widespread use of the "*Day Planner*", operational planning is probably the most common and well known type of planning. But it represents only one way to plan. There are actually four current levels of operational planning in the real world. Each level represents our progressive ability to control our lives in a way that brings *holistic value*. Holistic value means we are getting a balance from the things out of life that matter most.

Moving up in the levels of operational planning represents also an upward mobility in the self-mastery triangle. The four levels start with a focus on controlling time and move upward into controlling one's self, thus evolving from time management to self-management.

Level I is the most basic of planning and involves making a list of things to do. It's comprised most of the time of notes and checklists. It recognizes the necessities that act upon a situation and creating a list seems to be an attempt to put some sort of order in that situation. But is mostly a product of the Reactive Zone. The demands are listed in the order of occurrence without considering priorities or importance. For example, if I write on my to-do list: 1. Buy groceries; 2. Pickup son from daycare; 3. Buy gas—the three chores apparently have the same importance. If I run out of gas, then I can't control the situation and therefore I'm acted upon, instead of being the one who acts.

Level II planning attempts to build upon level one by putting the required things on a time frame, as in posting activities on calendar. While this is an essential part of planning itself alone is not yet enough for we still haven't considered our values and priorities (in the example above, it does not matter if I put the three chores on today's calendar after work, it still does not prioritize things and if I run out of gas my day is still ruined). If we want to move to a higher ground of success and control in our lives we need to do something different.

Level III planning is by far the most familiar and popular method of operational planning. It captures everything that's good in the previous two levels of planning and it also takes a big step forward. It enters the sphere of values and priorities. This is how it works: first we decide on the core values that we'll live our lives by. These values are the attributes we want to be recognized for. They are the quintessential principles that we will govern our lives by and are the highlights and characteristics that will be talked about after we're gone. Once we've established these values, the next step is to write down short term (less than one year) and long term (over one year) goals. With values and goals established, level III planning helps us prioritize our daily tasks. (If I first buy gas, then I won't run the danger of getting stuck; this allows me to accomplish the rest of the list, so *I CONTROL* the rest of the day). The real key to success in this level is thinking of proactive activities that will bring us closer to fulfilling our goals. These activities will be consistent with the values, the short term and long term goals already written down. We then prioritize our actions using a simple prioritizing system, based on importance (or whatever criterion we deem necessary at the time).

Once the priorities are set, we'll use level II planning to place the priorities on a calendar (or daily schedule).

This is important, because it increases focus which translates into staying productive. Also it drives itself, by providing a small feeling of accomplishment as we reach the end of each priority. This sense of accomplishment fulfills a core human need that can motivate us to complete more tasks in the allotted time.

Despite this obvious leap forward in level III planning there are still some drawbacks which prevent the achievement of total control and true success. It does not address the different roles we play, leaving huge gaps in our lives that go unrecognized and therefore are unplanned for. Because we are focused on daily tasks, we may easily be getting lost in reactivity while engaged in level III planning. This is caused by the limited view achieved by looking through a daily window, and thus clouding our global perspective and killing our ability to see how our daily tasks are helping us achieve our short and long term goals.

Level IV planning has emerged as a result of this situation to provide a holistic method of planning. It incorporates all of the benefits of the previous three levels. However, it adds a dimension left out so far. It addresses roles in our lives. Each of us plans different roles at different times. We are parents, civic leaders, volunteers, managers, etc. It's also within these roles that many of our reactive activities creep in.

Level IV planning is about taking time to complete the best proactive activities for the many different roles we play. It also confers an escape from the reactivity of daily planning. Instead it focuses on the week. Looking at our roles and priorities in term of a week or a month creates a broader perspective. This also allows us to focus on the most important things first.

Tactical Planning

If you have been serving in the military, are just a chess player or like to watch old war movies you certainly know that tactical planning is the skill of using all available means to accomplish an end. In tactical planning the horizon is from a few months to a few years. Tactical planning can be broken down into two components:

1.   **Project Planning.** Whereas operational planning is used to manage and gain control of our everyday lives, project planning helps assure success of the projects we are responsible for. The project per se can be anything. The key is that project planning can help assure the project is finished properly and on time and that everyone is kept up to date on its progress. Project planning differs from functional planning. Project plans use what is called a Gantt chart. (*6)

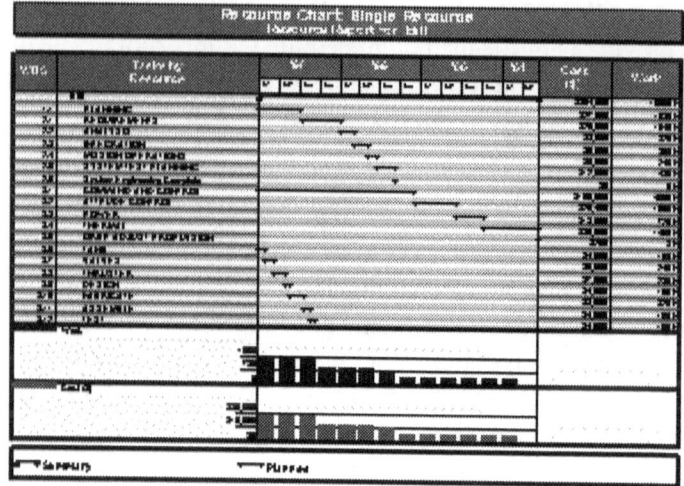

There are three main components of a Gantt chart:

- ❖ Time line. It provides either a completion date (in its simplest form) or visual mapping of how the project will progress over time.

- ❖ Task line. This tells what task is to be completed

- ❖ Assignment line. This shows who is responsible for completing the task

So why it is so important to take time to complete a project plan? There are many reasons of which hereunder are enumerated the main five:

- ❖ Communication

- ❖ Trust

- ❖ Focus

- ❖ Ownership

- ❖ Control

Project planning enhances and increases *communication*. By assigning each task and providing a timeline for its completion a boat load of questions and/or a lot of confusion is eliminated. Everyone involved in the project knows what needs to be done, who is doing it and when it needs to be completed—that's the essence of effective communication.

A spin-off from the communicating ability of a Gantt chart is *trust*, because it conveys the idea of organized environment and a degree of sophistication. It relieves any doubt that the work will be completed properly. Nothing communicates competence more than a well organized person who has anticipated every contingency and has a well thought out plan. Providing a project plan for the work ahead is an excellent way to exceed customers' expectations and communicate a relationship of trust.

The following example depicts project planning through the use of a Gantt chart. Imagine taking this chart in your customer's office and discussing it with him. Can you imagine what such a presentation may say about you and the company you represent? Firstly it communicates that you're very organized. Secondly, that you have a vision and you're going somewhere. Thirdly it shows that you are a sophisticated professional who deserves respect, because with this plan you've just communicated a high probability of success.

Along with trust, project planning creates *focus*, which is the fuel for productivity. It is the power to get things accomplished. A Gantt chart provides the team with clear responsibilities and clear expectations for the time frame of the completions of each task. Project planning implicitly creates *ownership*. Because the name of the responsible party is written down on the Gantt chart, that party is responsible for reporting on the completion date. This internal motivator helps team members complete their assignments timely and in a quality fashion.

Control is another aspect of proper project planning. With this all mapped out and ownership of the tasks assigned, the progress of the whole shebang can be monitored much more easily and efficiently.

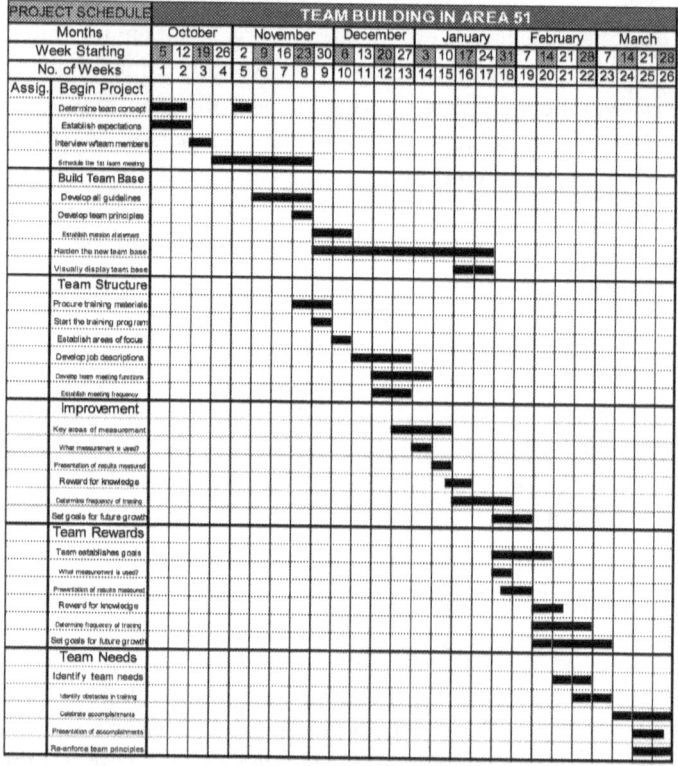

2.   **Crisis Planning** is when things go wrong. It represents project planning but with a twist. The same components and formats of project planning are employed, but the objective of the crisis planning is to eliminate a defect, to restore quality to the job or service and to regain customer's confidence. By providing your customer with a crisis plan when the quality of service went South (or for that matter providing

your boss with one when you encounter a defect in the process), you restore their confidence in your abilities and you give them visual reinforcement that everything will be taken care of. After all, "Errare humanum est" (Latin dictum meaning *to err is human*). The very act of presenting this plan will convey reassurance of your commitment for solving the problem and that everything is under control.

Strategic Planning

Strategic planning is looking through a window towards a planning horizon of several years to 10 years or more (*1). Companies use strategic planning to determine in which direction the company should go. A typical strategic plan may include what markets the company wants to penetrate, or it may include topics of growth, specializing or technology updating. Strategic plans give the overall vision of where the company is going.

For the individual, strategic planning might include the long-term goals and values within the self-mastery triangle. It may include where they want to be personally, professionally or financially. It requires *written goals*.

Writing realistic, achievable and worthwhile goals is not easy, but is obtainable. Below are a few tips for S.M.A.R.T.S. goal writing:

- ❖ *Specific*—The goals need to be specific and attainable.

- ❖ Too many people make their goals too general ("I want to be famous!") or shoot for the stars.

- ❖ Sometimes they have the tendency to write more than a goal within a goal. "I'll exercise today!" versus "I'll swim 10 pool laps today after work!" is a good example here.

- ❖ *Measurable*—To be measurable the goals need to be expressed in specific quantified forms (see the above example of a specific goal).

❖ *Aligned*—It means that the goals are worthwhile and that they fulfill a specific need or desire. It also means that they are in sync with personal values and purpose.

❖ *Reachable*—In order for the goals to be reachable they must be realistic.

❖ It is not realistic to set a goal to climb Mt. Everest next week when the last time you walked more than the distance from your office to your car was 10 years ago when you had a flat and your wheel wrench was the only missing thing from your trunk.

❖ So the first step is to make sure the goals are challenging but not too far above one's own capacity.

❖ It also means to ask if you're the only one that the goal depends on. If the answer is "yes" then the goal is reachable.

❖ *Time*—Make the goal time bound. This creates a target to shoot for. It gives accountability for reaching that goal. Accountability creates motivation that naturally drives the actions towards achieving the goal.

❖ *Stretched*—The goal should stretch the performer beyond past performance and beyond the usual zone of comfort.

Organize

Organization is another ingredient that is essential in management. Proper organization means to take all the variables and give them structures to follow. Organization also simplifies effectiveness and improves efficiency. For example, by bundling job duties with team member responsibilities the work is organized more efficiently. This may be oversimplification but look at the principle behind it. The key to organizing is to group and classify in the most logical manner so that the resources are used efficiently. There is though a demarcation line beyond which too much organization becomes cumbersome and therefore inefficient. Organizational problems appear when people are too far ahead or too far behind this line. Organizing involves three steps, as depicted in the following Good Management Flowchart:

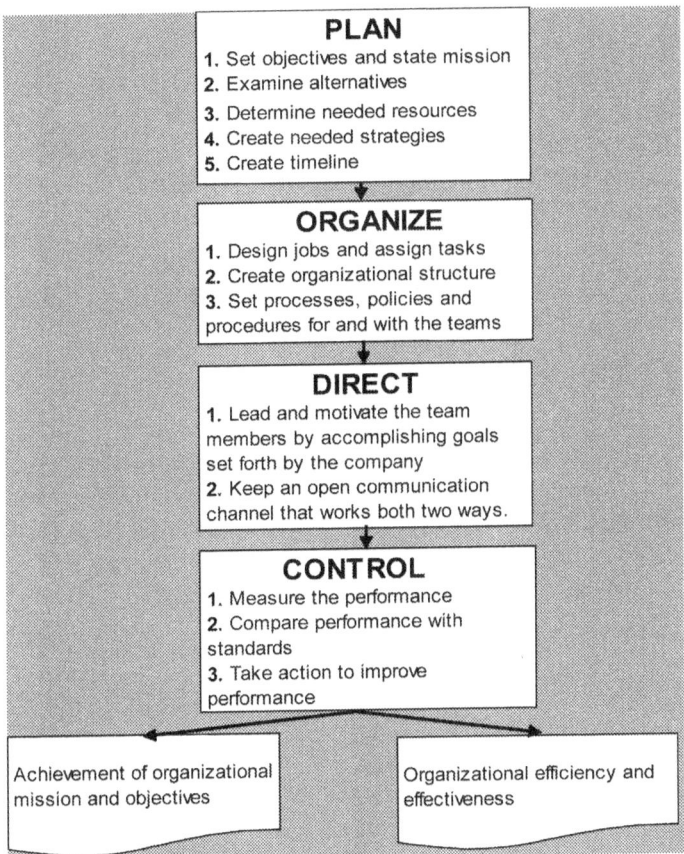

Design Jobs and Assign Tasks

For a site to run self-sufficiently, all the needed tasks must be organized into job duties and responsibilities for each of the team members.

To have something be self-sufficient it means that the people need to actually be involved. They have to feel ownership of their work. This means enlarging the job duties beyond the bare-bones requirements of a particular specialty itself. It means sharing and providing opportunity for all team members to fulfill leadership responsibilities adequate with their capabilities.

Create Organizational Structure

Let's say that the strategic plan calls for creating an Overall Quality Model environment. The Overall Quality Model environment is the structure that must be created and organized for any endeavor to be successful. Overall Quality Model provides the involvement, the tools and the means which organize the team members into continuously improving persons.

Set processes, policies and procedures

The next task in organizing is to determine how the work flows. To do this, each step is organized in a flowchart. The flowchart uses visual symbols to display the logical steps team members need to take in order to complete a task in the most efficient manner possible (see fig. 16 for an example of a process flowchart).

Direct

Successful modern managers *direct* their associates toward self-direction.

Directing is more than just pointing a finger in the direction one should go. It involves providing a road map for those involved in the team, along with the attitudes, emotions and actions necessary along the way. Will they be directed towards reaching a win-win environment? Will they be using the right attitudes? These are the kind of questions that need to be asked all the time when directing.

To direct we need to keep the end in mind and not loose sight of it ever. It takes a broad vision to properly direct. A good director promotes innovation by making team members feel comfortable about being heard. The good director does not care who takes the credit for innovative ideas and does not fear the success of others; s/he will willingly and readily clear the way for any and all team members to grow and succeed.

Lead and motivate

A good director is the motivator. The directing manager will want that all the attitudes, emotions and actions of the team members to lead towards positive achievement of the priory set goals and objectives.

The first focus in leading and motivating people should be *to get them to do something because they want to.* To accomplish this you must find out what their needs and wants are and then mold and shape the task so that it meets and fulfills these needs. Say you want someone to monitor safety as part of your direction to increase ownership on the job. So, instead of commandeering: "from now on I want you to be responsible for the following..." you may need to first realize that feeling important is a basic need of all human beings. So you need to mold the new responsibility to meet this fundamental need. You need to have a personal interview with the person intended for the new task and explain using sincerity how important s/he is to the team. You then tell him/her how impressed you and that you believe s/he can fulfill an important mission. You explain the opportunities s/he will have by embarking in this new role and the good things s/he will start being involved in. Most people want to do a good job; they just need encouragement, acknowledgement and a feeling of importance to unleash their work initiative, sense of loyalty, and their dependability.

Communicate openly

Frequent communication *in both directions* is essential for proper directing. An airliner captain is in constant communication with air traffic controllers along the way, otherwise it'll be disastrous. Everyone needs feedback on how they are doing. Team members need to constantly know if they are going in the right direction. The best way to give them feedback is to observe them doing something good and then acknowledge their positive behavior. The more you do this, the more they will move in the direction you want. However, if your purpose is to catch them doing something wrong and acknowledge only mistakes, they may feel discouraged thinking that they'll never be able to move in your direction.

Control

The managers are in control by knowing where they are *at all times.* Being in control should not be limited to just the financial aspect of the management job. Good managers will maintain control in all aspects of their activities.

There are several systems designed for controlling processes. Budgets and time cards are intended to control labor; check sheets to control processes; inspections to control quality. An effective manager has a control process for everything and involves heavily all the team members in the process of control. By maintaining control managers show to their customer, their teammates and to the top brass that they are willing to prevent problems from occurring, rather than simply addressing them as they occur.

Monitor and Measure Performance

This is without any doubt the most important, but often the most neglected aspect of the process of control. Monitoring and measuring performance is an act of prevention and falls into the category of important but not urgent (proactive zone). It is a natural tendency to put the things that are urgent ahead of the ones that are not. However, when those things that are important are pushed onto the back burner, the whole idea of prevention is undermined and the activity starts to take place in the fluctuating zone rather than in the proactive one.

We monitor and measure by creating quick and convenient ways of collecting data. To monitor labor, we may use automated time clocks; to monitor motivation we may use periodic team meetings; to measure customer satisfaction we may employ customer surveys. Whatever we device, the key is that these means of monitoring have to be used frequently and consistently because they are the lens through which our operation is captured. The day you abdicate the frequent and consistent use of your monitoring lens is the day you immerse yourself in darkness; you simply cannot know what's going on in your operation if you're in the dark.

Once the pertinent data on your operation is received, you must devise a means of measuring it, to see how it stacks up, to see what effect has on the whole operation. After that it needs to be visually displayed so that all the team members can see their progress, their success and check if their team falls behind. By doing this you make the performance matter. You are telling your associates that it is important to perform in those areas that are measured. Human beings want to perform (it is a core human need) and therefore you are telling them that their time and dedication are worthwhile.

Compare Performance with Standards

When visually displaying these measured performances, make sure *there is a generally accepted standard to compare to,* otherwise the display is meaningless. There are industry standards that can be adopted; there are financial standards that each company puts forth; there are marketing standards that the strategic plan points to. Whatever the standard is, it needs to be clearly defined to avoid any misunderstanding or false hope.

Take Necessary Action to Improve Performance

To control effectively, the processes need to be self-sufficient. When a process breaks down, usually there is a good reason for that.

One of the key steps of controlling is to make changes in the conditions that caused the process to fail. The pure definition of insanity is to do the same thing over and over, expecting a different outcome.

We need to ask ourselves:

1) Is the process punishing? If any step in the process is inconvenient or even punishing, people tend to avoid doing it or devise shortcuts. To overcome this situation, just make the process simpler and the steps more convenient for those involved.

2) Does the performance matter? If following the process does not matter, people will put it off and gravitate around things that do. So make things matter. Establish positive consequences to occur when the process is followed and repercussions when it is not followed. *It needs to be frequent accountability and people need to feel important* for following the process. Also the process itself needs to be made important to follow.

FRONT LINE MANAGEMENT

The front line manager in a service-oriented business is the facilitator. The manager facilitates the following two aspects of his/her job duties:

❖ The fulfillment of the company's tactical plan in accordance with established long term strategy set forth by the company's executive leadership.

❖ Creation and growth of an Overall Quality Management environment.

To facilitate these two areas means to help their associates, their distributors and their customers align their goals and actions with fulfilling the long-term plans and in the same time to establish an Overall Quality Model environment in their area of activity and responsibility. It means inoculating these goals into the prevention cycle so that front line are planning, organizing, directing and controlling the actions that lead to these goals.

The Fulfillment of the Tactical Plan

To accomplish this, managers need to set goals, make plans and then work the plans. Since their time is divided between accomplishing the objectives of customer satisfaction, operational effectiveness, financial performance and marketing, goals and plans need to be made for each of these four areas.

A worthy goal for any manager is establishing processes for preventing defects in the service. A defect is considered anything that hinders the achievement of the tactical objectives according with the preset strategy, such as, for example a promised service that was either missed or forgotten (customer satisfaction), improperly maintained equipment (operational effectiveness), too much absenteeism which leads to overtime and over-budget direct labor (financial performance) or being too caught up in the daily operations and not showing up for a pre-bid meeting (marketing).

By preventing defects in service managers reduce the amount of crisis management needed.

A crisis acts upon managers and forces them to act and in the same time it perpetuates other crisis. When a manager works hard to "put out a fire" this takes his/her focus away from the other areas of responsibility and this lack of focus in planning, organizing, directing and controlling breeds new "fires". The more defects can be prevented, the more time is available for working on important but not urgent matters, like for example keeping the prevention cycle turning.

While in your planning and organizing stages of your management activity, go ahead and establish processes for accomplishing each of the objectives from the tactical plan enumerated prior. Create a process for eliminating missed service. Create a process for preventative maintenance of equipment; create a process of staying in budget, etc. By establishing logical steps for completing each task you can focus on one issue at a time: first making sure that all the team members are trained on the processes and then assuring that steps are followed. This is much easier and streamlined, inducing much less stress and creating higher job satisfaction than constantly "fighting fires" by you becoming the process itself (becoming the fire fighting process). The processes are similar with the intricate mechanism of a Swiss watch. Each cog serves a precise purpose and all work together for only one purpose—to tell the time.

In any process several actions are combined to achieve a result. For processes to be successful, those involved in them must experience these job satisfiers:

❖ A feeling that the job is important and that it matters

❖ A sentiment of self-achievement by those involved in the processes

❖ A notion of recognition

❖ A sense of responsibility

❖ A measure of accountability

❖ A feeling of accomplishment and personal growth

If we go back to the watch analogy we see that once all the cogs are in place, the wearer needs only to supply power (wind it) and adjust the display as needed. As long as the wearer does this, the correct time is always displayed.

Processes work in a similar fashion. The managers who, for example, want improved quality will get improved quality as long as they supply the power (motivation) and make the necessary adjustments (re-tuning of the process, discipline, retraining, etc.) when or as needed. The power comes from a constant and consistent presence of job satisfiers.

As managers learn to balance their efforts in all areas of responsibility and learn to work within the prevention cycle they will see that old problems inherited or previously created begin to disappear and more time is freed to work more comfortably within the cycle.

Creation and Growth of an Overall Quality Model Environment

Managers create and grow an Overall Quality Model environment for the simple reason that the purpose of the Overall Quality Model is to yield a stable environment where strategic targets are more easily reached.

Beginning with the empowerment of all the team members, managers using Overall Quality Model principles get people involved. Involvement creates commitment and ownership in working towards continuously improving quality of service. This environment allows teams to actively work on shortening process duration with improved customer satisfaction and increased financial rewards. It also leads to reduction in turnover, complaints, fire-fighting and much more.

A visual example of the traditional approach to management in comparison with the pro-active approach theorized in this text is represented further. The industry this model pertains to is the building services industry.

Typical Management Style in the Building Services Industry:

DISTRICT

- AREA
  - BUILDING
    - **Area Manager is the center of:**
      - ✓ Quality Assurance
      - ✓ Problem solving
      - ✓ Motivation
      - ✓ Regulation
      - ✓ Discipline
      - ✓ Supplies
      - ✓ Equipment
  - BUILDING
    - **Area Manager is the center of:**
      - ✓ Quality Assurance
      - ✓ Problem solving
      - ✓ Motivation
      - ✓ Regulation
      - ✓ Discipline

✓ Supplies

✓ Equipment

METHOD OF CONTROL: REACTIVE AND ANACHRONISTIC

Because the area manager takes over employees' responsibilities and their self-reliance there is a constant friction and a crisis management mode. The area manager has to permanently chase the needs, wants and problems of the unempowered employees.

Management Using the Overall Quality Model Principles:

DISTRICT

- AREA
  - o BUILDING
    - Area Manager is the center of:
      - ✓ Quality Assurance
      - ✓ Problem solving
      - ✓ Motivation
      - ✓ Regulation
      - ✓ Discipline
      - ✓ Supplies
      - ✓ Equipment
  - o BUILDING
    - Area Manager is the center of:
      - ✓ Quality Assurance
      - ✓ Problem solving
      - ✓ Motivation
      - ✓ Regulation
      - ✓ Discipline
      - ✓ Supplies

✓ Equipment

METHOD OF CONTROL: PRO-ACTIVE APPROACH

The area manager is the:

- ✓ Planner
- ✓ Organizer
- ✓ Director
- ✓ Controller
- ✓ Facilitator
- ✓ Mentor
- ✓ Trainer
- ✓ Provider
- ✓ Process Manager
- ✓ Acknowledger and Praiser/Motivator

As it can be easily seen, within the reactive approach there is a multitude of antagonistic activities that germinate and thrive, because the method of control is inadequate. In an Overall Quality Model environment every team member plays a role and carries responsibility in the work process. Their responsibilities go beyond their strict specialty duties encompassing monitoring and measurement tasks, inherent with the prevention process.

People who learn to work in a team receive responsibility and authority to act and in turn are more able to resolve quality or other matters before they become issues. The team is geared to work towards zero defects in service as they continuously rely on their strengths and recognize opportunities along the way. As they craft accomplishments they increase the level of confidence associated with their product and pretty soon they take full ownership of their work.

At this point they become the center of responsibility for their own success. Conversely, the manager then moves out of the center and watches the trends, acting more like a coach by encouraging, nurturing and making minute adjustments in the newly created and self-sufficient Overall Quality Model environment.

Primary Responsibilities of Front Line Management

Any discussion on front line management responsibilities needs first to address three factors that make or break a service company: *the customer, the team members and the budget.*

The Customer

Managers need to start with a "Can Do" attitude all of the time. It does not matter if they don't yet know how to complete the required project at the time. The important thing is that the customer knows that whatever the issue, they can come to you for they know that you'll find a way to accomplish the project.

However, once you say you'll do it, you need to keep your commitment and find the best way to produce the expected result.

Also, managers need to possess a "Value-Added Mentality" The focus on value-added services is just as important as the attitude displayed. Value-added means becoming customer-oriented. The customer perceives the company in the image its manager projects. Management needs to always be professional when dealing with customers keeping in mind on one hand the golden rule that (with some minor exceptions which confirm the rule) "The Customer Is Always Right"; and on the other hand gently reiterating the guidelines of the contract when their expectations become exorbitant.

Open communication with the customer is another crucial aspect of dealing with and tending to the needs of the customer. Problems tend to get out of hand and issues multiply fast when nobody's communicating.

The customer hears mostly negative comments about your service which often stick in their subconscious mind and then work against you in the long run. It does not matter how small the problems are, if the negative remarks continue to build up due to lack of communication their perception is that you do a terrible job regardless of the true reality in the field. The reality might be that overall there are only insignificant problems and that the service provided is good.

The only way to eliminate the negative remarks from the customer's mind is proper communication. Communication is eliminating the negative effects because the manager has a timely response and a *solution* (as opposed to an *excuse*) to a negative remark.

It is the difference between a job and a career: spending your time to draw a paycheck or turning the time into self-fulfillment and satisfaction. In management is always the way you *put yourself across*. It's about making a difference. (*7)

Quality Control is one good example and the way it is managed and communicated across says a lot about customer-oriented professionalism.

The Team Members

Like the customer side of the equation, an equal amount of attention needs to be conferred to forming self-directed teams. Managers should think of team members as customers. If they are perceived that way managers will work just as hard to retain them. Managers will though employ several ides in their quest to team stability.

❖   *Training and certification* of team members is one of these responsibilities. This will require coaching and mentoring. When people understand what to do and get trained on how to do it properly they work better, faster and efficient, becoming more productive. Training reduces stress because people are less likely to make costly mistakes. Training, supporting, acknowledging and rewarding those who follow the training becomes the most important part of the training process because people will be more likely to repeat the learned behaviors in the future.

❖   *Empowerment* is the opportunity given to people to act instead of being acted upon. It's the freedom to select choices and make decisions; to take on responsibility and authority; to be allowed self-reliance and to be involved in decision-making that affect the environment. This means giving team members responsibilities within the framework of their job position and allowing them to participate in decisions related to those responsibilities. Empowered team members work together cohesively, producing zero defects. Under empowerment the available workforce turns from people just bumping along seeking a paycheck to people satisfying needs of self-esteem, self-achievement and advancement. It is after all the front line manager's job to facilitate that.

❖   *Motivation* comes in many forms. Many think of it as primarily monetary rewards. Although money can be a powerful motivator, it is not necessarily the strongest one. *"If you work just for money, you'll never make it, but if you love what you're doing and you always put the customer first, success will be yours"* was one of McDonalds Corporation founder Arthur (Ray) Kroc's favorite quote (*8).

The most powerful motivators are the *job satisfiers* represented below:

- o   Recognition
- o   Feeling of Importance
- o   Responsibility
- o   Achievement

- o Acknowledgement
- o Involvement
- o Appreciation
- o Praise
- o Opportunity
- o Trust
- o Support
- o Feedback
- o Friendly Atmosphere

It's important that a manager earnestly and sincerely seeks to nurture these satisfiers in team members. Without them a manager will be plagued with dissatisfaction, turnover, and low productivity. Job satisfiers are most effective when they are frequent and consistent. Waiting to praise someone at the semiannual review won't drive today's performance. Job satisfiers need to be part of the manager's character and they must be utilized at every encounter with the team members.

❖   Managers are *Providers* of the necessities that their teams require to be successful in their job. Besides job satisfiers, they need to be provided with the *tools and equipment* that make their work easier. Failure to fulfill this responsibility undermines all of the motivational techniques used.

The Budget

If managers fail to satisfy the customer's need then the customer will go elsewhere for service resulting in loss of business; if managers fail to satisfy the needs of a team, there won't be anyone left to produce; and if they won't satisfy the budget requirements there will be no business at all. Balance is crucial to survival and success. The budget is as important as the customer and the team. It is obvious that by staying in budget a profit is created which in turn provides the life blood of the company itself.

This brings us full circle to the financial performance. Profits are generated to accomplish all the other strategic objectives.

When the profit created exceeds the projected profit, it should be analyzed in the same manner a loss would. An excessive profit may mean that something else is out of balance and later down the road this imbalance will hurt the future results. Or it may mean that an increase of productivity and efficiency was created, in which case the situation is extremely proactive and it might be possible to pass on to the customer some of the extra profit. This will in turn create a more satisfied customer, who will spread the word within the industry and thus producing more opportunity.

Methods used in the budget activity:

❖   Control—Profits are made by being in control. Effective systems of control help monitoring costs so that expenditures can be adjusted before they erode the budgeted profit. Setting up a control process is absolutely essential for achieving the operational targets and to meet tactical objectives. Good financial control improves the ability to monitor budgets, balance expenses and produce the projected profit that was budgeted for the period. There are a number of budget-control tools available but the more the teammates are involved in the control process, the more commitment towards following it results. Some ideas for teammates to get involved might be the following:

- o Making a team member responsible for designing and posting a remainder flyer.
- o Having the members of the team set production goals below the budgeted time.

o Designating a team member to be responsible for monitoring and measuring the team's production rates. Have a quick report on previous day's hours before each shift. Provide visual charting posted for the findings.

❖   Budget standards—A budget needs to be set for each day, week, month and year. Subsequently the variable costs need to be periodically reported and discussed. These reports and the manager's ability to make real time adjustments when the reports are out of line will determine the gradient of success in making a profit.

Work Schedule

Another important responsibility of front line management is the creating, controlling and organizing the *Work Schedule.*

The front line manager's work schedule needs to *shadow* the schedule of all the working teams that are managed—leaving enough time during the normal business for administrative chores, for completing paperwork or for running errands. Managers need to take in consideration the geography of their area of responsibility, keeping focus on ergonomics. In *controlling* the daily work schedule, a great approach is prevention. A great preventative measure is to let others know what the manager's schedule is and provide a protocol to follow if team members need to get in touch. This piece of information allows individual team members to make other choices within their area of expertise and in line with their level of empowerment before they call for advice. This situation minimizes stress and the time spent on the phone (not important but urgent activity, characteristic for the Fluctuating Zone).

THE OVERALL QUALITY MANAGEMENT MODEL

The Overall Quality Management model is a long term management style that focuses on quality and customer service. Overall Quality Model involves everyone in the organization and uses means of measurement called metrics to monitor team activity for continuous progress.

Overall Quality Model changes attitudes and adjusts the way people are perceived. An Overall Quality Model style respects the dignity of human beings by calling and treating employees as associates, team members or specialists. In contrast, the traditional management style views people as workers, subordinates or employees. Such a view acts as an invisible barrier to people who could contribute on a greater scale.

In Overall Quality Model leaders from the top down are committed to the main idea that everyone in the workplace is valuable, everyone is a resource and all people are capable of improving themselves, the organization within which they operate, and the product (in this case service) provided to the customer. Overall Quality Model puts everyone on a level playing field so that intimidation is eliminated and nothing can smother creativity and innovation.

There are four fundamental components that act as a base of Overall Quality Model:

1) Team member empowerment and self-directed work teams

2) A zero defect standard achieved through the activity of prevention

3) Continuous team improvement

4) Continuous process improvement

These ingredients allow for an environment where everyone in the organization can truly reach peak performance and create an organization that is dedicated to quality and customer satisfaction.

Team Member Empowerment and Self-Directed Work Teams

Overall Quality Model is a participatory management concept that considers an empowered team to be capable of accomplishing and producing more than any one individual; where the final result of all the team members working together is greater than the mere sum of all of the individual contributions. Basically the Overall Quality Model is the framework that helps growth in management and its very structure supports a culture that automatically fulfills the core human needs of the team members involved in the work process and those of the buying consumer, or the customer. This is the whole force behind the Overall Quality Model, and the self-directed work teams and the empowerment simply make a perfect match between organizations and the methods used for motivating their people to achieve success.

Empowerment means giving a person or a team the necessary information and then allowing the freedom to make choices and decisions within the framework established by the company and based on the information provided. It's the ability to act instead of being acted upon; it's being accountable for decisions; it's creating responsibility and authority so that individuals can develop self-reliance and be involved in decisions that affect their environment. Creating empowered and effective self-directed work teams is one of the most rewarding achievements for a manager. By forming *self-directed work teams* a perfect culture is created which drives elevation in others. Each team member plays a role on the team through which the individual receives recognition, praise and a feeling of importance. Each person has the opportunity to participate in leading the group, which helps them stretch their capabilities. People with low self-esteem or immature on the personal level can become self-reliant and productive when correct principles of empowerment and need fulfillment are used in relegating them.

Empowerment does not mean the loss or the abdication of authority, decision making ability or power; it means exercising the authority to help others in controlling themselves. The decision making ability stays the same and still remains the manager's property but by allowing input from the team this ability is increased. That is because people who are dwelling within the Overall Quality Model environment think independently, are proactive, have a clear vision of accomplishing goals and put priorities first.

An empowered workforce significantly reduces turnover and reduces administrative duties as well, freeing managers to work in the Pro-Active Zone, so that they can turn their actions towards prevention, facilitating empowerment, and managing the Overall Quality Model environment.

One key to empowerment is learning to think empowered. The traditional workplace is geared towards catching the wrongdoing and systems or processes are designed this way. Managers and supervisors control what goes into the group and what comes out, there's a hierarchy system for making decisions, for giving orders and for completing tasks. This hierarchical system rewards individual achievements, enticing all persons in a lead role to guard their position and turf. This situation denies the common worker the responsibility, involvement, authority, sense of achievement or importance, rendering them powerless and throwing them into the Reactive Zone.

Successful people are pro-active and empowerment through Overall Quality Model is all about working proactively. When managers and team members work proactively they increase their ability to act on their own and instead of reacting to un-empowered people, they use their time planning and organizing or making decisions.

Important tasks that are not urgent such as building relationships careful planning or training are put off by reactive managers whereas a proactive person puts these activities at the top of their priorities. The net result is that problems inherent with the reactive zone start to disappear in a proactive state.

Empowerment evolves over time. It takes awhile for people to change their old paradigms and some people may even resist responsibility. It's more convenient to receive orders than to accept responsibility for own decisions. Those who expect instant gratification from empowerment are usually discourages and frustrated. On the other hand, those who understand the evolution of empowerment and prepare for it can expect quantum leaps in performance once the empowerment takes hold in their operations.

Zero Defects Standard

An Overall Quality Model environment demands zero defects in any part of an operation. If problems can be prevented from occurring then there's a significant reduction in issues that impact an operation, and it is the pure essence of prevention. As with everything else, the achievement of zero defects requires a process, which involves several steps:

❖   Step 1—Monitoring and Controlling of Gathered Data. Achieving zero defects standard requires careful observation of the work processes or habits that exist. The goal here is to advance the existing power of process awareness so that nothing unobserved would be capable of sneaking in. The information gathering helps red-flag any potential problem and empowers the team to make decisions based on facts rather than opinions.

❖ Step 2—Translation of Data into a Visual Presentation. Once the data is collected, the team measures the results by translating it into a graph which makes problems stand out from the rest of the information. The use of Information System capabilities is justified and encouraged here and the application of technology can pay big dividends in isolating negative trends before they become problems (preventing them from becoming big issues). The graphs make it easy to present the data at team meetings and in the same time graphs motivate, by illustrating the progress made.

❖ Step 3—verify if a process is out of alignment. The graph will indicate where opportunities for improvement exist. If an opportunity crops up then a process is out of alignment. The team needs to decide if they have all the facts and unanimously need to act upon the situation to bring about the needed improvement.

❖ Step 4—Brainstorm solutions and then implement them unequivocally. The team thus finds solutions for the opportunity of improvement and then everyone needs to buy into the solution and implement it without hesitation. Responsibility for the implementation project needs to be divided up and the team should use a Gantt chart to schedule the project and to monitor its progress.

Continuous Team Improvement

The Overall Quality Model concept requires focus on effectiveness. This is achieved by constantly practicing and refreshing those skills that hone and enhance the team members' abilities and by frequently measuring the performance of the team. It requires a standardized certification process for all the team members in their individual job positions.

Teams also can tell if a process is out of alignment by constantly monitoring and measuring their own performance. This whole system of measurement, evaluation, education and implementation assures that the team is constantly improving and it is working in the proactive zone.

Process Improvement

Process improvement implies process management where the system is broken down into smaller measurable components, meaning that every task is broken down into actions which help assure that the task is completed properly and with zero defects. Once a process is established for each task and the appropriate specialists are trained then teams turn their focus on processes instead of people. If something eventually goes wrong, the teammates don't blame each other but rather look together at debugging the process.

Effects of an Overall Quality Model Environment

❖ Reduced Costs. As each team member starts to focus on their specialty, they learn ways to improve efficiency and effectiveness. They increase prevention also and this brings along a significant operational cost reduction by eliminating (or at least reducing) costly repairs or rework.

❖ Competitive Edge. As a result of involvement and job satisfiers, employees tend to become more loyal and the adverse effect of turnover is reduced.

❖ Improved effectiveness. Along with specialization in their jobs, working in a team environment allows the quicker identification and resolution of any problem

❖ Improved Customer Satisfaction. As each team member becomes more involved their desires, motivation and commitment will inevitably increase. This creates an increased quality for the customers who will have a better response time for their requests.

❖ Increased Revenue. All of the above results combine to increase the revenue because of the possibility to pass some of the savings to the customer or because these savings allow for providing value-added services or activities.

CHAPTER IV

CUSTOMER SERVICE

"Coming together is a beginning.
Keeping together is progress.
Working together is success".
Henry Ford,
Founder of Ford Motor Company

Steven Anthony Ballmer, Chief Executive Officer of Microsoft Corporation affirmed that *"We can believe that we know where the world should go. But unless we're in touch with our customers, our model of the world can diverge from reality. There's no substitute for innovation, of course, but innovation is no substitute for being in touch, either"* (*8). Successfully interacting with customers requires artful skills. The art of customer service is no secret—it is simply the ability to influence people. When talking about influencing people, we step out of the management boundaries and enter the leadership zone.

What's the difference between management and leadership?

When in "management mode" we think "be efficient"; we cut a step in a process which results in efficiency, or we complete tasks quickly; we're resourceful and efficient with our budgets and complete paperwork ahead of time. In all these examples we use as reference the objects of our trade (budgets, time, tasks, etc.). To extrapolate, management is the art of being efficient with *objects.*

However, if we apply a management perspective to dealing with people, we may be efficient in handling a situation, saving time or managing budgets. But dealing with people is much more than that, in a totally different context. It is totally different than dealing with things, because things don't come with emotions or core human needs like people do. Things lack the complexity of human self-esteem, whereas people are complex creatures of emotion. The key here is to be *effective* with people.

Being efficient with people creates indifference, resentment, frustration, even anger.

Stepping beyond efficiency and into leadership means that we are willing to pay the price, to sacrifice time and efficiency to be effective with people.

Therefore, the answer to the aforementioned question is that in management we are *efficient with things* whereas with leadership we are *effective with people.*

Being effective takes time. A leadership perspective pays the price to build relationships of trust, in order to influence people. Leaders always think first about how they can influence others. Only after that they start thinking in terms of time and efficiency.

Most of the objectives of a service company deal with the ability to effectively interact and associate with people. They also deal with the ability to influence people. For example, when providing value-added services it is imperiously necessary to know how to effectively present the work in a way that the customers will recognize the benefit they are receiving. Only then the bond with the customer grows stronger.

To create win-win partnerships with the customer requires the knowledge of how to effectively meet human core needs. This is dependent upon the ability to use good people skills. A partnership involves two or more parties that work together interpersonally to solve each other's problems and to meet each other's needs so that there is a win-win situation in every aspect of their collaboration. Otherwise a partnership will never synergize.

Excellent customer service evolves from four human relations laws.

1. **Perfect inter-personal skills** that spring from principles like integrity, honesty and kindness. By learning to communicate often and at a higher interpersonal level you will influence others. This creates trust.

2. **Meet and maintain customer's core human needs.** This is a relationship builder. People will trust you more if they perceive that you are looking out for their best interest.

3. **Exceed expectations.** This ability creates satisfaction and confidence. By raising your own bar above the customer's level provides peace of mind and a cushioning margin for when things go wrong.

4. **Build character.** Principles like integrity, honesty, kindness and others must be at your own core. Working at the personal stage makes you trustworthy and helps with follow-through.

As management professionals, our primary objectives need to gravitate around perfecting the above principles. This way, as our character evolves, the interpersonal skills will get more consistent and will have more power. We will know how to influence people in their best interest. That's what leadership is all about.

You need to sow the seeds of interpersonal thoughts to harvest interpersonal actions. Like everything else in life, customer service must be learned and reinforced periodically. The refinement of skills is much like the refinement of knowledge expressed in the formula for growth in Chapter II. It is called the "*Principle of Execution*".

The Principle of Execution is the ability to execute a plan, a skill or a behavior when it counts. In management, what makes the difference between success and failure is how well the team executes the plan. Perfect execution comes from constantly learning and practicing correct skills and principles.

Customer service skills become obscure and forgotten if the importance of constantly maintaining and improving them is neglected.

The principle of execution applies just as much in being inter-personally effective as in any other aspect of life. Skills and knowledge never come in a complete genetic package. They are left to our undertaking to be honed and refined.

Examples of this principle can be easily identified in the world of sports, where great successes are derived from hard work, constant refinement and endless practice.

No one seeking victory is exempt from the grinding stone; everyone needs to obey the principle of execution.

To the same extent, professional managers learn correct principles and practice them until they are executed perfectly. It is not far fetched to assume that your entire job depends on your customer. Below are some cold hard facts about the customer, which emphasize the importance of customer service:

Fact 1: It costs five times more to find a new customer than it does to retain an existing one. It takes long marketing hours, resources, not to mention the initial costs of start-up.

Fact 2: It takes an average of twelve positive encounters to overcome a negative one. This fact underscores the importance of principle of execution. Doing it right the first time and all the time is a valuable time saver, a great customer retainer and profit generator. Doing it right the first time takes practice and self-discipline.

Fact 3: The average person will tell eleven people of an unsatisfactory service. Then each of the eleven will tell an average of five other people and thirteen percent of them will tell twenty people or more. Furthermore, some statistics reveal that word of mouth is the strongest form of advertisement.

Fact 4: Sixty-eight percent of customers who terminate their business relationship with a service provider do so because of dissatisfaction with the response to their needs. The key here is finding out what customer satisfaction means to them. Because the customers come from different environments, their expectations and needs may vary significantly. It is possible to make up for a substandard expectation but when a need is violated, the result in most cases is termination of contract.

Fact 5: Of customers who take time to complain, up to seventy percent of them would come back again if their complaints were resolved. This percentage increases to ninety-five if the complaint was resolved quickly. The quick response to a complaint provides the customer with a feeling of importance. Immediate resolution to an issue maintains the basic human need of self-esteem and creates satisfaction.

Fact 6: Satisfied customers tend to be more lenient when a defect arises. This is due to the fact that most people will avoid beating down a known performer. The caveat is that past performance won't last long if the defect in service is not eliminated soon and quality is not restored.

Customer service requires people skills. But before attempting anything in this area it pays to have a thorough understanding of human expectations and needs.

Distinct customers will have varying expectations but each of them will have roughly the same needs as all humans require. The success as a manager relies on the ability to form strong relationships with the customer.

Here's a model for creating strong relationships:

1. Learn and meet general expectations

2. Discover customer's specific expectations

3. Exceed expectations through value-added service

4. Fulfill and maintain customer's core human needs

Customer Expectations

Customer expectations may transcend the specifications of the contract or in some cases exceed or fall short of the specifications. This is because expectations are formed from environments and experiences people encompassed throughout their entire life. Each of these expectations is born from internal standards that form throughout the life. The customers either consciously or unconsciously evaluate the level of service every time they have an encounter. From their internal standards comes out a set of expectations according to which they will judge the services received. This is called customer perception. The customers see their internal standards as the truth, so no matter what the service provider's own perceptions are if the customer perception differs the result is a loss. Understanding the customer's general and specific expectations is important because it forms the foundation that must be laid prior to start building an enduring relationship.

This is where value comes in. A customer will cease or retain a service contract based upon the value created throughout a contractor's relationship.

Fortunately we can influence relationships. As we progress, stagnate or regress in the relationship model we increase, freeze or decrease value to the relationship.

When managers fail to meet the general expectations of their customers they create a deficit in their relationship value. The general expectations represent the contractual specifications, augmented with the unwritten "Customer Bill of Rights".

A summary of these rights is presented below:

❖ The customer has the right to *common courtesy*. This implies:

  o politeness

- o respect
- o consideration
- o friendliness
- o looking professional
- o taking care of customer's property
❖ The customer has the right to *easy access*.
  - o easy access to management
  - o convenient hours to receive service
❖ The customer has the right to *responsiveness*.
  - o prompt call backs from management
  - o speedy resolutions for any concerns
  - o full attention attributed to their problems
❖ The customer has the right to *reliable service*.
  - o consistent performance
  - o performing right the first time
  - o integrity in completing contracted assignments
  - o accurate billing

Many managers are good at merely meeting the general expectations. The problem inherent with this is that the value in the relationship is zero, because meeting the general expectations is assumed by every customer. There is a multitude of other competitors out there who can meet these general needs. In the customer's eye this situation makes you indistinguishable from the competition.

The secret here is to stand out by becoming a "*person of value*." We live in a capitalistic society and capital is derived from Latin "capita" which means head. In relations with the customer, it means the excess value "per head" or "per service" the managers create but don't get paid (*9); it means to go the extra mile.

Value in a relationship is crated when we begin to exceed the customer's general expectations by addressing their specific expectations. Specific expectations are commonly known as personal preferences or perceptions. As individuals we see them as truths but they may not seem like a truth to someone else.

Professional managers will learn their customers' expectations and how they perceive quality.

Value-Added Service

General and specific expectations can only be exceeded through value-added services. They are services provided over and above the contract and are tailored to meet customers' specific needs. Although every person is different, studies have shown that the average customer values service in the following order:

1. Quality
2. Availability
3. Knowledge of the persons they are dealing with
4. Ease of doing business
5. Support services
6. Performance
7. Follow-through
8. Price

This reveals that customers value more the possibility of their expectations being exceeded than mere price.

There are two principles that can be used to exceed these expectations:

❖ *Principle of overwhelming.*—In the beginning of the middle ages, the Mongolian conqueror Genghis Khan's fame and strength was founded on the principle of overwhelming. His ability to exceed his enemies' expectations brought fear in those he sought to conquer. He used overwhelming organization, discipline and maneuverability in his military campaigns. Because the principle of overwhelming is a true natural law it works in forging strong professional relationships. Exceeding expectations is more a function of leadership than management. A manager may be inclined to meet only the general expectations because the efficiency paradigm won't allow any margin for *exceeding* expectations. "It takes too much time!" or "I don't have the budget for it!" may be what a manager says when confronted with exceeding expectations. However, the leader is focused on influencing people and will go the extra mile in planning and organizing, so that the desired outcome is assured. Because there are so few real leaders, so few people are really exceeding expectations. Let's glance at a few actions leaders can take to exceed expectations:

o Constant flow of professionally presented ideas that help improve customers' operations

o Professional looking project plans by using Gantt charts

o Professional appearance of the whole team

o Written processes and documentation

o A professional, formal training program and certification

o Frequent customer updating through visual presentations that show the benefit and value of the extra service provided

o Self-directed teams who are involved on a more sophisticated level

o Mounted job aids and posters that project to the customers what the management stands for.

o Frequent use of thank you notes, holiday and birthday cards.

❖ *Principle of Small Things.* This principle is an extension of the principle of overwhelming because it adds to the overwhelming effect and is the absolute epitome of leadership. It is not the big birthday present that strengthens the bond between friends but rather the small things. What really builds enduring friendships and long lasting relationships is the small and thoughtful actions. It's the praise we give; it's the avoidance of criticism, and so on. These are small things but great outcome results when they become a part of our thought process, actions, and eventually our character. Building relationships with customers is no different.

If managers want to add real value to a customer relationship they need to bring uncompromised dedication. Fulfilling core human needs is the consistent performance of simple and seemingly small actions. A manager looking through a leadership perspective will eventually learn everything that is necessary about the need of fulfillment.

Value-added services can become commonplace and over time these services begin to recede from the customers' consciousness. Time and consistency have a way of making things commonplace. In psychology this phenomenon is referred to as adaptation. Adaptation is a physical and psychological process in which we get used to something and only when a circumstance changes we do realize that we became used to it.

The building services industry is highly prone to adaptation. Services that were considered value-added a while ago are generally forgotten and expected as commonplace at present. How can this situation be avoided? First, avoid telling the customer outright. This method is less effective than, say, marketing the extra services through subtle reminders. Good managers sell what they're doing. A good way to do this is listing of all value-added services and presenting them to the customer for satisfaction rating. This reminds the customer that the value-added service is over-and-above the contractual stipulations and thus it eliminates adaptation. Another ides is to send a customer a "symbolic" invoice for all the value-added services and mark them "no charge".

Whatever the method, good managers will always market or remind their customers of the value-added services that they are providing.

The Difference between Expectations and Needs

The next step in creating valuable and strong relationships is the fulfillment and maintaining of core human needs. What's the difference between expectations and needs? While expectations are rooted in the conscious mind (remember, they are formed from exterior environments and experiences encompassed throughout the entire life), the needs come from a much deeper source—the subconscious mind. Therefore, needs are more universal than expectations to all human beings because the needs affect our self-identities or our sense of self-worth. The stronger the emotions involved with a situation, the greater the capacity to affect human behavior.

Violating a customer's needs can result in anger or resentment because their entire structure of self-esteem is challenged.

Below is a summarized depiction of the differences between customers' expectations and needs:

EXPECTATIONS:

- Conscious
- Specific
- Surface
- Short term

"Desires outcome from the service encounter"

If you dissatisfy your customer by not meeting their basic *expectations* you can still recover.

NEEDS:
- Unconscious
- Global
- Deep
- Long term

"Desires outcome from being human"

If you dissatisfy your customers by not meeting their basic *needs* you will loose them for ever.

Needs

Knowing human psychology and behavior can help build enduring relationships with customers. It also helps in influencing people to do things because they want to do them. Used the right way this knowledge helps increase effectiveness and productivity in management.

Meeting someone's human needs is probably one of the most significant actions a manager can carry out. It's so important that it is used by marketers when selling things.

Our needs for esteem and self-fulfillment affect who we believe ourselves to be. By fulfilling the needs of others we foster or catalyze internal motivators within these other people.

The internal motivators drive these people to greater levels of effectiveness, higher levels of self-worth and help them cling to your relationship. The reverse side of this medal is that when you violate core human needs, it can rot or destroy the relationship.

Human behavior is influenced through people seeking need gratification. Psychologist Abraham Maslow is known for establishing the theory of a hierarchy of needs, writing that human beings are motivated by unsatisfied needs, and that certain lower needs need to be satisfied before higher needs can be satisfied. In reality most people try to satisfy several needs at a time. Maslow's Hierarchy of Needs (*10) is exemplified below:

- Self-Actualization
- Esteem
- Love
- Safety
- Physiological

Maslow studied exemplary people such as Albert Einstein, Jane Addams, Eleanor Roosevelt, and Frederick Douglas. According to Maslow, there are general types of needs (physiological, safety, love and esteem) that must be satisfied before a person can act unselfishly. He called these needs "deficiency needs." As long as we are motivated to satisfy these cravings, we are moving towards growth, toward self-actualization. Satisfying needs is healthy; blocking gratification makes us sick or evil. In other words, we are all "*needs junkies*" with cravings that must be satisfied and should be satisfied (*11).

Physiological Needs
Physiological needs are the very basic needs such as air, water, food, sleep, sex, etc. When these needs are not satisfied we may feel sickness, irritation, pain, discomfort, etc. These feelings motivate us to alleviate them as soon as possible to establish homeostasis. Once they are alleviated, we may think about other things.

For a customer, these needs are met by default.

Safety Needs

Safety needs have to do with establishing stability and consistency in a chaotic world. These needs are mostly psychological in nature. We need the security of a home and family. However, if a family is dysfunctional, (i.e., an abusive spouse) the other spouse cannot move to the next level because of the constant concern for own safety. Love and belongingness have to wait until the abused person is no longer cringing in fear. Many in our society cry out for law and order because they do not feel safe enough to go for a walk in their neighborhood. Many people, particularly those in the inner cities, unfortunately, are stuck at this level. In addition, safety needs sometimes motivate people to be religious. Religions comfort us with the promise of a safe and secure place after we die and leave the insecurity of this world.

This is a need that can be indirectly fulfilled for the customer by offering freedom and stability from the unexpected. This can be accomplished by:

- ❖ Providing a stable operative environment that allows the customer not to worry

- ❖ Providing a process that allows the customer to be sure that the work is being completed properly

- ❖ Educate and consult the customer on the status and the progress of the work

Like expectations, human needs are prone to adaptation. This means that the fulfillment of them may not earn you bonus points but failing to do so will significantly reduce the strength customer gives to your relationship.

Managers who fail to maintain safety needs will eventually loose the customer.

Social Needs

Love and belongingness are next on the ladder. Humans have a desire to belong to groups: clubs, work groups, religious groups, family, gangs, etc. We need to feel socially loved by others, to be accepted by others. Performers appreciate applause. We need to be needed.

Other needs in this category are the need for giving and the need for friendship.

Generally these needs are met by the customer's family, personal friends and social groups. But there are many people who seek friendship and belongingness at work. These tendencies can be identified through these tips:

> ❖ The customer frequently enjoys talking about issues non-related to the work at hand.

> ❖ The customer has many pictures at the office displaying personal interactions with other coworkers.

Esteem Needs

There are two types of esteem needs. First is self-esteem which results from competence or from the mastery of a task. Second, there's the attention and recognition that comes from others. This is similar to the belongingness level; however, wanting admiration has to do with the need for power. Here are some other needs that fall in this category:

> ❖ The need to feel important, which is at the same level with the aforementioned need for attention and recognition.

> ❖ The need for self-achievement

> ❖ The need for acknowledgement

Out of all needs, esteem needs have the most significant universal affect on people—most importantly the customer. Regardless of the situation, we all seek the fulfillment of this need. If we make others feel important and needed, we'll not only be well liked but we'll create relationships that last and that are successful. Just as important, the consequences of ignoring this need are a relationship breaker. Ignoring or even violating esteem needs lead to the creation of indifference, avoidance, resentment, dislike, anger or hate from the people with whom there's a relationship or association. Of course, the degree of the negative reaction to this un-fulfillment depends of the other person.

The truth is that nobody wants to look stupid in front of other people. Somehow we think that our self-worth is diminished when other people acknowledge and validate our shortcomings in front of others. The customer is no different. To assure that the customer's need for esteem is never violated, a series of questions should be frequently asked, such as:

❖ Do we create conditions that would make the customers feel stupid in their eyes or in the eyes of others?

❖ Does our management style ever create situations where the customers could be embarrassed?

❖ Do we give sincere appreciation for our customers' services or advices?

❖ Through our actions, do we make the customers feel important?

Self-Actualization

The need for self-actualization is "the desire to become more and more what one is, to become everything that one is capable of becoming"(*10). People who have everything can maximize their potential. They can seek knowledge, peace, esthetic experiences, self-fulfillment and oneness with God, etc. They become motivated merely by doing the best job possible. People who are self-actualized want freedom and independence. They are motivated when they are provided with an environment where self-directed work may occur. Most of the customers will have self-actualized needs. As a manager you may not be able to fulfill these needs. The key is to not violate this need for self-actualization. Some ideas that work in this respect are presented below.

- ❖ If a customer brings up operational or procedural ideas for management, *never reject them.* Compliment and commend the customer for the advice and if you deem that there's some merit in the suggestion, try to work with it and implement whatever fits your process.

- ❖ If a customer wants a service to be performed a certain way, *do not reject the request; add to it.* If you think that it won't work, find a diplomatic way to make suggestions but do not reject it!

How to work on the development of inter-personal skills is beyond the scope of this text. Nevertheless, a good source that can be used for interpersonal skills development is Dale Carnegie's best seller work titled "How to Win Friends and Influence People". This book has sold over fifteen million copies since its first publication in 1936 (yes, almost three quarters of a century ago, and *it still is* the benchmark in this domain); the principles used in this book are universal and transcend time, race, religion, etc. They are enduring principles that have been passed down through time due to their powerful effect on human behavior. They are the key to unlock the interpersonal relationships (*12).

There's though an aspect of inter-personal skills that need mentioned here and that's more often than not ignored in manager' interaction with their customers: non-verbal communication. It affects managers even before the first word has been spoken because more often than anyone may think, it conveys the *unintended* message.

BODY LANGUAGE

It can be considered as any communication that is not verbal or written. What managers say is not as important as how they say it. Most of their words will be lost in the conversation but the body gestures will have a huge impact on the customer's attitude and perception. By using the body language properly and effectively managers can enable their customer to interpret the message the way it was intended to be perceived. At the University of Southern California, Dr. Mehrabian's studies indicate that body language accounts for 55% of how a spoken message is interpreted. The next most important factor, according to Dr. Mehrabian, is "vocal qualities"—not the words per se but rather the tone, the timbre, the intonation and the pace of delivery. These accounted for 38% of the speech's effectiveness. Therefore, 93% of the effectiveness of a verbal communication has nothing to do with the meaning of the words. The words themselves accounted for only 7% of the effectiveness of a speech (*7).

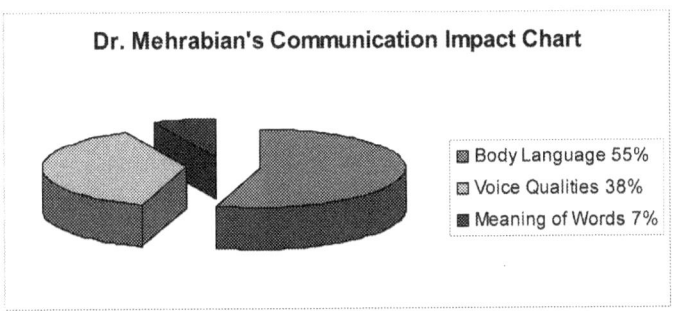

Dr. Mehrabian's Communication Impact Chart

Body Language 55%
Voice Qualities 38%
Meaning of Words 7%

We already have established that most communication takes place on a nonverbal level. In other words, most of the messages communicated to the listener are based upon information obtained from nonverbal cues given by the sender. In most situations, we react to what we think a person "means" more than to the words that are said. A major source of confusion is the inconsistency of what is said with the meaning derived from factors such as facial expression, body language, tone of voice, touch, time and distance.

Body language used during communication can be an invaluable tool in maintaining the accuracy of the message that you are sending; but, surprisingly, most people rarely learn how to read it. Kinesics is the study of nonverbal communication, namely eye contact, facial expression, gestures and body movements. Body language plays a major role in communication because it is continuous and usually more reliable than verbal communication.

For body language to communicate a positive message, eye contact at an appropriate eye level, smiling sincerely and the occasional nod to acknowledge attentiveness must occur during the conversation. Eye contact lends a perception of sincerity to the interaction and reinforces that the subject matter under discussion still is important. Continuous scowling without a periodic smile or expression of warmth can attach a cold and dispassionate feeling to the message.

Positive gestures, such as good posture and composed body positioning (shoulders straight, non-fidgeting) can enhance the precision of verbal meaning and reinforce the attention and retention of the communication. Repetitive illustrators, such as hand positioning and movements that compliment a verbal message, can increase the persuasiveness of the message, although too many hand gestures will become a distraction. Adaptors (unconscious self touching), such as chin or brow rubbing and repetitive hand or arm scratching, can decrease the persuasiveness of a message.

Body language is just as important for the listener as it is for the speaker. When the listener exhibits infrequent eye contact, shifting body weight from one hip to another, sighing and fidgeting, the speaker may interpret the actions as a feeling of insignificance and indifference for the communicated message. We also look to posture to provide cues about the communicator, such as confidence, aggressiveness, fear, guilt or anxiety. Many gestures, such as how we hold our hands or the strength injected into a handshake can reflect the same information; however, cultural differences can lead to misinterpretation of these gestures (*18).

Facial Expression and Gestures

Facial expressions can confuse or counterbalance spoken words. We usually read the speaker's face to interpret what they say and feel which is why communication may be partially blocked when speaking and listening to someone wearing dark glasses or sunglasses. It is extremely important, especially in a professional environment, that a speaker use facial expressions that are congruent with his message.

Shifting eyes away from the listener frequently while speaking can foster distrust. Another facial expression that can interrupt or change the message sent is laughing or giggling while speaking about serious or important subjects. Given the amount of serious information discussed, a customer can interpret any of these as a feeling of undue irrelevance assigned by the manager.

Touching

Haptics, tactile or touching nonverbal communicators, can take on many forms and convey different meanings. Accidental touching, which can take place in a crowded room or elevator, elicits an immediate and usually-defensive response of maintaining or increasing the zone of comfort. Social touching—ranging from a handshake to a pat on the back or an arm around the shoulder, which takes place during an expression of concern or giving advice—usually is interpreted and received appropriately by the customer or by team members, but occasionally can be perceived as undue sympathy or pity.

Comfort Zones

Most of us tend to feel a bit uncomfortable when someone is standing too close. The comfort zone is the area of space around an individual that is private territory. For Americans and most Western cultures, the four zones of interpersonal space are:

- ❖ *Intimate space*—direct contact up to 2 feet—close relationships and healthcare professionals who bathe, feed, dress and perform phlebotomy procedures.

- ❖ *Personal space*—2 to 4 feet—interactions among family and friends.

- ❖ *Social space*—4 to 12 feet—most interactions of everyday life and business.

- ❖ *Public space*—more than 12 feet—lectures, speeches, and similar presentations.

Children tend to have a wider comfort zone that usually narrows with maturity (*15).

Use of Time as Nonverbal Communication

The use of time can communicate our perceptions of personal status and importance relative to others. Sending a message of limited time or taking one's time can be useful in effective communication. Generally, nonverbal cues can affect the meaning of the words that we speak in five ways, listed in Table 1 below (*14).

Table 1

Effect of Nonverbal Cues	
Repetition	repeating the verbal message
Contradiction	contradict the verbal message
Substitution	substitute for a verbal message (e.g., widening of eyes communicates a more vivid message of fear)
Complement	add to verbal message (e.g., a pat on the back in addition to verbalized praise)
Accent	underline a verbal message (e.g., pounding the table)

Many nonverbal factors can contribute to the message that is actually sent in an interaction. Although the interpretation of nonverbal cues is culturally based, effective managers use them appropriately to enhance communication.

Active Listening

Hearing is a physical ability, while listening is a skill. Another component of effective communication is the art of listening, known as active listening. The manager often is engaged in communication for the purpose of soliciting information (e.g., pertinent information regarding a complaint) and active listening skills can ensure that the needed key information will be obtained and subsequently documented accordingly. Table 2 below lists some tips for active listening.

Table 2

Tips for Active Listening	
Maintain eye contact	Look at the speaker.
Stop talking	Don't interrupt the speaker.
Stand/sit still	Maintain a body state that reflects attentiveness.
Nod your head	Physical validation to show understanding
Lean slightly toward the speaker	Physical validation of interest/importance
Check for understanding	Repeat information and ask questions for clarification.
Focus on the content/message	Refrain from judgments of the person or emotion.
Respond with interest to the message	Avoid defensive or judgmental reactions.
Pay attention to body language	Look for body states that indicate illness or danger.

Active Listening Barriers

A few factors can obstruct active listening for even the most skilled manager. Factors such as personal bias, prejudice, language differences and accents, actual noise, negative attitude and distracting mannerisms or clothing all can impede active listening. Additionally, the inability to maintain attention span and emotional states such as worry, fear, anger and defensiveness also can adversely affect active listening skills.

Using active listening skills demonstrates to the customer that you are paying attention. Most people can mentally process words faster than they can speak them; therefore, to actively listen, concentration and focus on the customer may help to keep the manager's attention from wandering. Although you may, in fact, be able to listen while looking down at the floor or up at the ceiling, this action may imply that you are *not* listening.

Managers who practice good listening skills also can become more productive, as these skills can facilitate the acquisition of vital information, allowing them to respond appropriately and therefore achieve desired results faster.

Maintain Consistency

The effective use of verbal and nonverbal communication and active listening skills are vital to ensuring that the intended message sent is the message received. What is said must be consistent with what is reflected in the nonverbal communication. Effective communication skills, such as smiling and good posture, begin on the approach to an interaction and keeping in mind that we do not get a second chance to make a first impression should help facilitate the use of positive nonverbal communication cues.

Getting and keeping the attention of the listener, sending and maintaining the integrity of the message, and achieving the listener's understanding of the message all are critical to the communication process.

How to Use Body Language to Diffuse Anger

How can body language be a useful tool in the manager's arsenal? One answer might be that it can be used to diffuse anger.

Here are some helpful hints:

1) Match and Mirror—Keeping it subtle, match the customer's body movements. Don't mimic the customer, but adopt similar gestures and postures.

2) Adjust the voice to the customer's—Match the intensity and speed of the customer's voice.

3) Get the customer in a "yes" (positive) mode by focusing on facts—Begin and end statements with phrases that ask for agreement, like "Would you agree?"

4) Empathize and Agree with the objections—Use statements like "I would be angry too if…" or "That is terrible…"—this shows empathy. Eliminate the adversarial relationship by agreeing to the complaint or objection. Shaw the customer that you're on the same side.

CHAPTER V

HUMAN NEEDS AND TEAM MEMBERS

"Customer needs have an unsettling way of not staying satisfied for very long".
Karl Albrecht, Management Consultant, Futurist, Speaker, Prolific Author

In Chapter IV it was explained that people are motivated through the fulfillment of needs and if you violate the needs of a customer, you will loose that customer. The same principle holds true with the team members. If you violate the needs of your team members, you will lose them in productivity, in ownership, in independence and eventually in employment.

For many of the team members, the basic survival (physiological) needs—food, clothing, shelter or safety needs—job stability, workplace safety (both physical and mental) are fulfilled by their managers when providing them with a job and therefore with a paycheck. Until these needs are met, the team members will not worry much about fulfilling higher needs. But after their basic needs are met managers need to be prepared for the greatest reward of all—to help their team members climb to the top of their higher needs—to move from dependence to independence and finally to interdependence, where they will work for and share into the success of the group.

Everyone has the ability to move up in these stages of need fulfillment. Unlocking someone's desires and will is the key to motivation.

It's been said that motivation comes from a safe buried deep within every team member and their managers can only provide the key.

True motivation comes from the individual; we can't motivate anyone outright, we can only provide *keys* for motivation. For managers, these keys represent the way they treat their people and the environment they create for their teams. If they treat their teammates with respect, trust, competency and intelligence, most of the teammates will act with respect, trust, competency and intelligence.

If management provides for their teams an environment of responsibility, involvement, accountability and so forth, they create the nourishment that everyone needs in order to climb towards self-fulfillment and independence.

Managers can increase production, loyalty retention and satisfaction more in one day by using these principles than in a lifetime of trying to force feed policies and procedures to their people through distrust and fear tactics.

Establishing a positive environment leads to the creation of job satisfiers. These satisfiers need to be present for people to achieve their greatest potential. If the job satisfiers are absent, the void becomes a vortex of dissatisfaction which leads to poor performance and high turnover.

Job Enlargement and Enrichment

These are two other forms of motivation that can be connected with need fulfillment.

Job enlargement involves the expansion of a number of tasks involved in a job. This provides variety for team members. When variety increases so does job satisfaction. Enlargement allows others to become involved in the larger part of the organization.

It's a principle of human nature that people feel committed to a process in direct proportion with their involvement in its creation and in its operation. Enlargement also allows for job satisfiers and need fulfillment to occur.

Job enrichment is much like enlargement. It involves redesigning jobs to provide teammates with more authority, challenges and self-achievement. Like job enlargement, enrichment helps teammates graduate from lower need groups to higher ones of esteem and self-fulfillment.

Money

Money can be a motivator but it is neither the most powerful nor an effective motivator. Money has to do more with the lower levels of need. The graph on the next page depicts that as people have their basic needs met and they ascend to higher needs, money loses its influence as a motivator.

The employees I had a chance to work with over the years rated monetary remuneration (pay rates) as being number five on the top motivators list, well ahead of for example appreciation for a job well done (their number one motivator), or involvement (their number two motivator). Curiously enough this was totally different that what the management thought. Management most of the time considers the money factor as the number one motivator—hence their haste to award bonuses or wage raises just to motivate someone to for example take on an added task or to perform a particular task that was either crucial or nobody wanted.

The following chart shows the management's perception of the order of importance for motivators to enhance morale versus the employees' perception:

Management's Perception of importance of motivators	Motivators	Employees' ranking of same motivators
1	High Wages	5
2	Job Security	4
3	Promotion Opportunity	7
4	Good Working Condition	9
5	Interesting Work	6
6	Loyalty of Supervisor	8
7	Discipline	10
8	Appreciation	1
9	Help with Personal Problems	3
10	Involvement	2

Fear as a Motivator

If people value their job or want to be promoted, fear is a powerful motivator. But fear is also the most destructive for long-term employment. Managers employing this tactic may get their way in the short run but soon enough things begin to self-destruct. Fear forces people to do things because they must. Over time this builds resentment, anger even hatred. The result is then obvious: lower productivity, job dissatisfaction, etc.

Although the skills for motivating people can have a powerful effect, they are merely superficial if they don't come from within the manager's character. Managers must use each skill with the strong belief that they want to *sincerely and genuinely* build and lift other people.

Peak Performance

In order to understand how to motivate people to attain peak performance we need to understand a bit more about human nature.

There are five fundamental check-off items that must be present (the first two) or need to be eliminated (the last three) for peak performance to occur. Below they are presented as questions that any manager needs to ask when it comes downright to getting someone to perform day in and day out.

- ✓ In presenting a task (or a job) or when working on one, does the task meet a need of the performer?
- ✓ Is the task (job) a matter of importance?
- ✓ Are there any walls that impede others from doing the task (job)?
- ✓ Are there any punishing circumstances for the worker if the task (job) is performed the way you want?
- ✓ Is there a more rewarding circumstance created by not performing the task (job)?

Before we can address the circumstances that lead to asking the aforementioned questions we must understand what it means to perform. Similar to other things in life, we often do not seem to notice something as general as performance until we consider that there is a gap between what we perceive to be good performance and what we encounter.

Everyone has different expectations for performance. There seems to be a fine line between *excessive performance* and *not enough*. For example a supervisor who manages in an autocratic style to a point that resembles despotism, may drive people into the ground using productivity and profit as ends to justify the means. This is a case of excessive performance even if the results obtained are (for a short period of time) spectacular.

This brings to mind the legendary Lee Iacocca. When assumed the presidency of Chrysler Corporation in 1979 he imposed his towering personality to discipline and whip the organization into shape. In his first couple of years Iacocca produced spectacular results and Chrysler became one of the most celebrated turnarounds in the industrial world. (*3)

Other managers may become part of the crew to such a degree that there is a *lack of leadership*. This is a case of not enough performance.

So how can we tell what peak performance is, or how do we tell if there's excessive or not enough performance? The answer is found in what is universally accepted as standards of performance. The standards impose a "hurdle" that we all must clear in order to arrive at the optimum level of performance the company has set a benchmark for.

There are two types of standards: they are *general* and *specific*.

The general standards delineate the company focus, and the generally accepted benchmark for the industry. The specific standards communicate how much to perform, by setting specific goals.

The goals depict the time line, the schedule or the methods, and an acceptable minimum quantifying level for performance. Specific standards should be written within the boundaries of the general standards and should be expressed as goals. As specified in Chapter II goals need to be realistic, measurable, worthwhile and written down (S.M.A.R.T.S.).

As a reminder, S.M.A.R.T.S. goals, is a savvy but simple tool for goal setting to establish your goals with an action plan in place to achieve them. Here's the formula:

- Specific: a written goal with all steps necessary to complete it.
- Measurable: you and others can see how you are progressing.
- Achievable: stretching but doable.
- Realistic: relying only on your own efforts.
- Targeted: a clear objective noting consequences and potential rewards.

- Stretched: push your limit and get out of your comfort zone

Your future is whatever you make it. Read your goals daily and as you achieve them, replace them with new dreams to keep your life interesting and yourself motivated to achieve whatever you want.

Preventing Performance Problems

Our goal as managers is to prevent performance problems before they can occur, but occasionally it is inevitable that they do occur. In both preventing and responding to problems, good managers will refer to the Peak Performance Flowchart presented below:

PEAK PERFORMANCE FLOWCHART

➢ DOES THE TASK MEET THE NEEDS OR WANTS OF THE PERFORMER?

- **YES.** Go to the next question
- **NO.** First meet the core human needs then discover specific needs through an interview or a questionnaire.

➢ IS THE TASK A MATTER OF IMPORTANCE?

- **YES.** Go to the next question
- **NO.** Evaluate the intensity of set expectations and presence/consistency of accountability

➢ ARE THERE ANY IMPEDING "WALLS"?

- **YES.** Remove all the perceived "walls".
- **NO.** Go to the next question

> ➢ IS THERE A PUNISHING CIRCUMSTANCE FOR DOING THE TASK?

- **YES.** Remove the punishing circumstance and add positive motivators.
- **NO.** Go to the next question

> ➢ IS IT MORE REWARDING *NOT TO PERFORM*?

- **YES.** Use a performance scale to weigh the existing positive and negative motivators. Remove the negative motivators and increase the positive ones.
- **NO.** Go to the next question

> ➢ IS THE PERSON CAPABLE OF PERFORMING??

- **YES.** You just turned the situation into a positive outcome.
- **NO.** Consider a change in personnel.

Let's examine this flowchart in more depth:

Does Task Meet the Needs or Wants of the Performer? One of the first things considered is whether the task meets the needs and wants of the person delegated to perform it. This is where all the need fulfillment knowledge pays off.

Instead of expecting a person to do something to comply with the authority associated with the management position, it is better to obey one of the most effective principles in the human nature: get people to do things because they want to.

Abraham Lincoln taught this and it is an intrinsic characteristic of the most successful people. What could be more effective?

Getting people to do something because they want to will eliminate all of the baggage that comes from forcing someone to comply. A score of factors are eliminated: resistance, resentment, apathy, low productivity, sabotage. In its place managers create an interest in the activity, motivation to accomplish it and a general awareness for what that individual is doing.

Being able to assess a people's needs and then shape their tasks to fulfill those needs is a real skill. So before asking someone to perform a task or if someone is already performing a task, it is best to ask yourself:

- ❖ How am I making this person feel important for completing the task?

- ❖ How am I showing this person that I appreciate him/her for completing the task?

- ❖ How am I providing recognition in front of his/her peers for the completion of the task?

- ❖ How am I involving the person in creating the task or deciding on how it should be performed?

- ❖ How is this person getting what s/he currently wants by completing the task?

It takes time and patience, but once mastered, the skill of meeting the needs of the performer will seem a very natural thing to do.

Is the Task a Matter of Importance? Human beings are creatures of convenience; we seek shortcuts; we design gismos to make things more convenient; we pursue comfort. We are creatures of convenience due to the kind of society we live in. We find ourselves bombarded with massive loads of information and we spend increasing time on the job.

When taken in consideration everything that occupies our time it is easy to see why we gravitate around the most convenient, most important and most urgent things; we simply don't have time for things that do not matter or do not affect us. To overcome the tendency to gravitate to the most convenient tasks we must make the intended task a matter of importance. This means that we need to consistently enforce consequences when performance *is* achieved and when it *is not*.

If a task lacks consequences it will be neglected because the performers do not have the necessary fuel to propel them forward in completing it.

There are two types of consequences that must be considered: positive and negative. The **positive consequences** are considered the most effective. Abraham Lincoln said that you can catch more flies with a drop of honey than with a gallon of bitter gal. Studies have shown that people who receive positive consequences for an action are more likely to repeat that behavior. Team members who are complimented on their interpersonal skills will likely repeat the behavior and thus becoming even more effective. A single positive consequence will do more to motivate a person than a hundred of negative consequences. This means that we need to get better at catching people doing something *right*.

Negative consequences fall under the *fear* motivator. They are things along the "*You'll lose your job if you don't perform*" line. Negative consequences are powerful and at times they should be used, but if they are used as a whip to keep people in line they'll deteriorate the conditions that need to be cultivated when seeking peak performance.

So what creates a matter of importance?

a. High Expectations. They need to be clearly and consistently expressed.

b. Give Example. You and the other managers need to set the example.

c. Accountability. There needs to be a process in place for consistent and frequent follow-up. Every improvement needs to be praised and every failure needs to be addressed with concern.

Are There Any Impeding Walls to Achieve Performance? Some walls or barriers span from ineffective management styles or personal fear of embarrassment. Walls include anything physical or psychological that impedes anyone to perform.

As managers seek peak performance so do their team members. But many times there is an invisible wall that impedes the team members from completing the task as it is desired. The funny thing is that more often than not these walls are minuscule, even silly when they are finally discovered. These walls are invisible because of a general blanket wording such as 'it's a training issue" or "s/he always behaves like that", or because of the failure to provide and clearly state the standards and the expectations.

Some other common walls are created by policies and procedures. For example if we give someone contradicting directions it may be a matter of a poor stated policy. Or if we manage by the cliché: "Do as I say not as I do" we build a procedural wall because our actions tell our people that what is not important for us to do, certainly it's not important enough for them to do as well.

An effective manager will take time and care to check for any walls that may be caused by procedures, policies or by own individual style of management.

Is There a Punishing Circumstance for Doing the Task? Many times we ask people to do things that result in a form of punishment. If this occurs, people will naturally avoid completing the task.

For example if you demand that someone finish a task on a weekend, you'll punish that person by not allowing him time with his family. The natural tendency here is to let the task unfinished and come up with all kinds of excuses as justification.

How can tasks punish? By being:

a. inconvenient

b. counterproductive to core human needs

c. a contributor in increasing the work load.

Effective managers will consider whether the task is punishing in any way. By doing this, they can remove the punishment and improve the conditions where peak performance can occur.

*Is It More Rewarding **Not To Perform** the Task?* Just as it is human nature to gravitate to the things that are the most convenient, it is also human nature to cleave to the things that are most rewarding. The only problem with this statement is that the word "reward" carries a monetary connotation. Although the reward could be monetary, it is often in the form of core need fulfillment.

The easy way to determine if it is more rewarding *not to perform* is to ask these questions:

✓ Are there any consequences to performing the task? If there are no satisfying consequences people will not do it.

✓ Are these consequences positive? Because if it is inconvenient, people will tend to avoid it.

After working through this flowcharted model and still seeing that there's no change in performance, then it needs to be determined if the person *is capable of performing*.

Ask the following questions:

✓ Is there a lack of skills?—If so, provide skill training

✓ Intellectual disparity with the task?—If this is the case, reassign the job.

✓ Personality problems?—Help the individuals discover themselves by being direct and tactful.

✓ Defective attitude?—Be direct with the person and in the same time respectful. Consider a change in personnel.

✓ Low self-will?—Be direct and consider a change.

All that was presented here touches only the surface of the subject of peak performance. Nevertheless it should assist managers in building an environment where true peak performance can be achieved.

However, the level of success achieved will be greatly determined by how well managers can carry out the peak performance analysis with their people. As they learn to identify the real problems behind poor or non-performance, they will be able to use creativity and self-will to help their team members perform at their optimum level.

The level of implementation of all that was learned here about peak performance will determine the level of productivity, turnover and loyalty achieved and if it all leads to happier work environments and a heftier bottom line.

CHAPTER VI

ACQUIRING THE
LEADERSHIP PERSPECTIVE

> "A leader is most effective when people barely know he exists.
> When his work is done, his aim fulfilled, his troops will feel they
> did it themselves".
> *Lao-tzu, 6th Century BC Chinese Philosopher, Founder of*
> *Taoism*

COMPETITIVE AND COMPOUND VALUE OF LEADERSHIP

The added value that *a leader*, as opposite to *a manager* creates is called *competitive value* and is defined as the quantity and quality of people and ideas created by the leadership.

The word *competitive* bears two meanings. The first meaning for competitive is wanting to win or defeat somebody or something. This definition seems to suggest that only one person or only one organization can win. In today's integrated work place cooperation and collaboration are essential for success. Companies poll their resources together and form tactical or strategic alliances or operational networks and therefore they create a win-win situation which helps them better compete in the marketplace or achieve a business status that gives them a strategic advantage over their competition. Unfortunately in some instances the word competitive when referred to an individual has negative connotation suggesting a "take-no-prisoners, winning-at-all-cost, and doing-what-ever-it-takes" philosophy.

The second definition of competitive carries a different meaning—it means to be attractive in value or worth, as in "competitive pricing" or "competitive offer". Competitive value is a combination of both definitions, except that we win by helping all stakeholders in the business activity win.

So, to be competitive means to be more attractive in value than others because the individual or the organization is worth more and can provide grater value to the consumer. When talking about people within an organization, competitive value means the sum of each individual's skills, talent, knowledge and attitudes plus all the other personal values brought in.

For an organization, competitive value means the totality of the talent, work processes, strategies, and business activities that the organization possesses or engages in. If the organization has the best talent, work processes and strategies, if it is involved in the best business activities and if all these are consistent and reinforce each other then the organization will be much more competitive and profitable than others.

Because the leadership is comprised of many things, hereunder leadership is simplified by dividing it into three objectives that are common to history's greatest leaders:

- ❖ Leaders constantly develop and prepare themselves

- ❖ Leaders constantly develop and prepare others

- ❖ Leaders constantly promote vision and empower others to greatness

Notice how the first objective deals with self-development. By building up yourself, you increase your level of competence and your ability. By learning and developing yourself, you increase your perspective on life be it at work, at home or at play. Your perspective broadens, allowing you to see the inter-connectivity and relationship between the decisions you make.

A broad perspective obtained through learning is where a vision is born. When you learn, you get ideas and enlightenment of how to do things more efficiently or how to bring yourself to a higher degree of effectiveness. If you neglect building yourself through learning, the ideas become scarce and come few and far apart, because it is a simple law of nature: you can't grow without first learning, developing and applying yourself.

You can't create competitive value with a management per-spective. A management perspective causes you to narrow your thinking down to efficiency and expediency. It also causes you to get hung up on how much time it takes or how much it will cost to buy new technology and to train or teach someone else. The management perspective is inherently short-term thinking.

The second objective states that a leader always develops and prepares other people. By developing other people, you are compounding the amount of leaders within an organization; you have more people who are thinking, building themselves, satisfying customers by providing great services. They, at their turn build others and execute performance at a higher level. It's called "leverage".

Leaders realize that when they build others and prepare them, they add leverage to their capacity to lead. Said Scott Adams, the famous cartoonist and creator of Dilbert: "*We must develop knowledge optimization initiatives to leverage our key learnings*".

Leverage is where *compound value* comes in. Essentially com-pounding value means that something of value increases or multiplies at a faster rate. For example when you build a leader within an organization, that leader will build leaders creating a multiplied value because it is very powerful to have several individuals or subordinates who are generating ideas, inspiring others to greatness. As the number of leaders increases, ideas, loyalty, commitment, flexibility for change, and flexibility for action begin to multiply or compound. The ultimate result of compounding value is the multiplication of financial value.

Leaders generate competitive and compound value to an organization; managers don't. That's why one leader is worth several managers. However, a leader who can manage is priceless. Today's economic climate asks for more exceptional managers who possess a leadership perspective. The formula for growth and success still requires efficiency and expediency. We just need to realize that efficiency and expediency go well with things; never with people. People require effectiveness.

The third leadership objective calls for promoting vision and empowering others to greatness. This objective is the propellant for leaders to achieve explosive success. It shows what happens when leaders are put in an empowered environment. Once people know how to act through the first two leadership objectives, the third one allows them to reach their maximum potential. Helping people reach their highest potential is what leadership is all about.

A true principle in the universe is that "(...) *intelligence cleaves unto intelligence; wisdom receives wisdom; truth embraces truth; virtue loves virtue; light cleaves unto light; mercy has compassion on mercy and claims her own; justice continues its course and claims its own; judgment goes before the face of him who sits upon the throne and governs and executes all things".* (*17) True leaders founded on excellence will cleave to companies that are founded on principles of excellence. True leaders, who are founded on action, will adhere to organizations which are empowered to act. Also true leaders will hire other leaders. The empowering environment that a leader creates will naturally attract other strong leaders. Strong leaders will continue to build themselves, build others and empower people to greatness.

Competitive and compound value applies to managers as well. People with a management perspective manage and hire followers. Managers who are low on the leadership scale will cleave unto people who will follow the system and follow the manager. These types of managers tend to not hire people who are energized with new ideas or with a tendency to rock the boat because these people threaten their control and their system of efficiency. These people in turn hire similar types of people and so on until the organization is filled with followers.

If this stage is achieved, the organization is a perfect example of mediocrity and will require a true leader in command who will have to start from scratch, "getting the right people on the bus, the wrong people off the bus and then, *together*, figure out where to take the bus"(*3).

Leadership Scale

Leadership either comes from natural abilities or through learning from a mentor who models true leadership. "Exnihilio" (Latin for "creating something from nothing") is not possible in leadership. Everyone has to develop their shills, even those who have natural abilities into leadership.

The majority of people are mentored into leadership. That should bring comfort to the rest of us mere mortals. If we lack natural leadership abilities, we at least have hope that we can accrue them by learning from a true leader.

On the other hand, if we have natural abilities, we can always improve by continually building ourselves and by watching other leaders in action.

So what is a leader? Some define a leader as a person who is in the lead. That is only partial true; there are many managers who lead (in profit, or in marketing, or whatever) but who still are not leaders, for management and leadership are not completely separate domains. The truth is that you can have management without any leadership but conversely you can't have leadership without some degree of management. That is because pure management is the early stage of leadership.

Let's have a glance at the representation of the leadership scale.

EMPOWERMENT LEVEL
20
19
18
INTER-PERSONAL LEVEL
17
15
14
13
PERSONAL LEVEL
12
11
10
9
CONTROL LEVEL
8
7
6
5
4
ACTION LEVEL
3
2
1
0…Follower

As it can be seen, management is the basics of good leadership and that's why, for example we can drive financial results from management. The overlapping between the management and leadership is important because it signifies that to be the best possible leaders it still requires being good managers. Being a 20 on the leadership scale means that someone can succeed in just about any position in which that individual is placed. It means that the individual has all the attributes necessary to be the type of leader that creates competitive and compound value. However, to reach the pinnacle of "Level V" leadership as described by Jim Collins (*3) it requires the embodiment of a paradoxical mix of personal humility and professional will.

Leaders at this level are ambitious first and foremost for the company, not themselves; they are almost fanatically driven to produce sustained results.

The Leadership Scale is though augmented with this new level, called "Level V Leadership", creating *The Leadership Model* depicted below. The first level in both management and leadership is the Action Level. Good managers are at least a "3" on the Leadership Scale. Desire, determination, initiative and discipline are necessary ingredients for strictly creating financial value. All managers and leaders need these attributes. A glance at *The Leadership Model* will determine that these attributes are not enough for creating greater financial value and ultimately generating competitive and compound value for the organization. It may be easy by just looking at the model to say that someone has all the attributes listed under the levels of leadership. However, each attribute is composed of many different qualities and actions. Success lies in understanding the details. The Leadership Model provides only generalities. A closer look will help assess someone's own true strengths and weaknesses.

Let's look in more detail at all the levels of this Leadership Model.

Leadership perspective—doing the right things (being effective)

LEVEL V LEADERSHIP

21	Embodiment of a paradoxical mix of personal humility and professional will

EMPOWERMENT LEVEL (Promote Vision and Inspire Others To Greatness)

20	Create opportunities for your team members to grow and advance
19	Create an atmosphere that empowers others to greatness and promotes vision
18	Create a team structure with your people

INTER-PERSONAL LEVEL (Build and Prepare Others)

17	Assess leadership capabilities of those around you
15	Create a learning atmosphere to foster personal growth
14	Commit other team members to a common purpose
13	Use communication to build up others

PERSONAL LEVEL (Build and Prepare Self)

12	Learn how to influence and motivate others
11	Learn and develop competencies
10	Build character through principles
9	Self-evaluate; use your self-will and creativity to make the necessary changes

Management Perspective - doing things right (being efficient)

CONTROL LEVEL

8	Accountability
7	Measurement
6	System and process development
5	Organization
4	Planning

ACTION LEVEL

3	Initiative and discipline
2	Determination
1	Desire
0	*Follower*

Understanding them will help with the self-evaluation of the current position on the model scale and at the same time will help determine if there's any competitive and compound value created for the employer's organization.

The Follower

Even followers can bring some value to an organization. They bring a value up to "1". Also leaders need to learn to be followers in some way. They need to allow themselves to be influenced so that they, as well as others can grow. However, a follower can't advance beyond "1" for a good reason: a follower doesn't have the desire, determination or initiative and discipline to move up on the Leadership Model's scale.

Nevertheless more often than not, followers are put in management positions. When this happens it's because managers are managing followers and they put people into positions primarily to have someone follow their direction or because they can't look beyond the short-term cost of paying more for a leader. When a follower is put in a leadership position such as supervisor or manager, inevitably problems start to crop up.

Here's how to recognize this situation:

- ❖ There's little or no unity among the people the individual is supposed to lead

- ❖ There is little or no organization. Work is completed as it comes.

- ❖ There is high turnover in the individual's team.

- ❖ There is little or no involvement among the team members.

- ❖ Employees are frustrated and dissatisfied with their jobs.

- ❖ There is never real progress; the vicious cycle of "fire fighting" is the status quo.

- ❖ There are never any ideas for change. The manager does what it's always being done.

- ❖ Employees don't feel as part of a greater purpose. They don't understand why their jobs are so important.

- ❖ The manager is consistently working 70-90 hours a week, merely keeping afloat.

- ❖ Training and development is low on the list of priorities.

- ❖ The manager does not take time for self-improvement.

❖ There is very little communication and follow-up happening.

❖ Tasks or projects are rarely planned out.

❖ No measure of performance.

❖ High number of customer complaints.

❖ There is little or no accountability.

❖ Processes are not written and are only discussed whet there's a problem.

❖ Budgets and Profit & Lost statements are rarely made or reviewed.

The list could go on and on. The behaviors listed above will become clear later in the manual when we'll discuss competencies. As an interesting remark, the above problems are typically blamed on the industry someone is in, which depicts another characteristic of a follower: they tend to explain problems with reactive excuses.

When a follower is in a leadership role, it is overwhelming and stressful work, because the follower receives no benefit from compounding value. In other words, the follower typically takes all the work upon himself. This situation hampers upon the capacity of growth. When reactive activities are high, the growth capacity is low.

Someone's position on the Leadership Model's scale determines that person's capacity to lead. People can't lead more that they can handle.

As people progress through the Leadership Model's scale, they will notice that they become inherently and naturally proactive. Leaders always work in the Proactive Zone (Chapter II).They always plan, organize, direct, empower and build relationships of trust; they always self-evaluate and in the meanwhile they also train and teach others. The reactive activities are barely showing up on the leaders' radar screen.

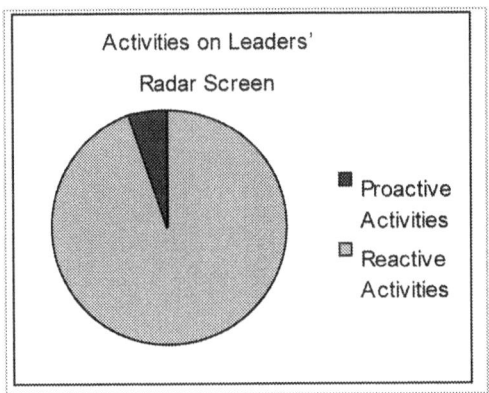

Sure, leaders have urgent things they must respond to, but these things are usually minimal. Leaders reduce reactive activities as they progress through each domain of the Leadership Model.

As pro-activity increases the level of stress drops dramatically. The stress a leader encounters in the Proactive Zone is a healthy, positive stress; it's the kind of stress that motivates rather than weakens. Healthy stress comes from the leader's performance. Since leaders are constantly proposing and developing new ideas and are taking on new projects, the added responsibility creates a positive stress. It comes from ownership for the success of the project. If the leader is at the Empowerment Level on the Leadership Model, the stress won't become negative because the leader has the benefit of compounding value to draw from. Because the leader has developed and empowered other leaders, the load can be safely shared. This also explains why the capacity for growth increases. It's that simple: instead of one person to handle the growth, the leader has produced several people worth spreading the growth over, therefore compounding the leader's ability and capacity to handle more.

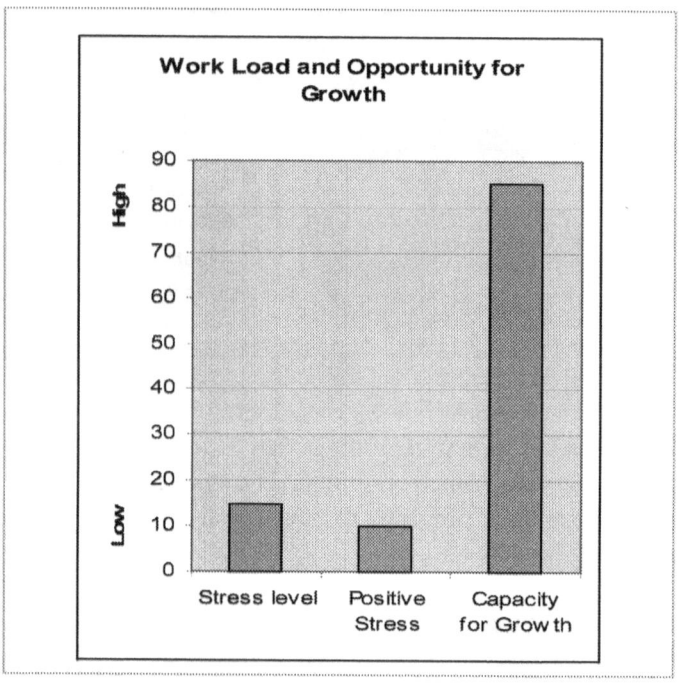

Understanding the impact of leadership on the work environment is a great way to know when the Empowerment Level is achieved and when a leader is able to decide on what opportunities to provide to subordinates. They just need to use the Leadership Model as a reference chart, for it is the standard against which performance can be consistently measured. By just pinpointing the level self-achieved on the Leadership Model chart it is possible to check the activities and the results that should be produced. The Model also depicts the activities and the results or the areas the emerging subordinate leaders should focus their efforts in.

For example, if you're in the Empowerment level and the manager you're developing is, say, in the Control level, you may want to reconsider giving the subordinate more responsibility.

Instead of responsibility as a form of opportunity, you can offer that person an opportunity to develop to a higher level on the Model. If you don't take the time to build before giving opportunity, followers or Action Level managers will be crushed under the weight of added responsibility for they simply lack the capacity and ability to support the added growth.

Understanding the outcomes from having a follower in a leadership position can assist you in helping your people pay the price to move up.

Action Level

When we move out of being a follower, we do so through desire, determination, initiative and discipline. These four human attributes are the foundation for excellent management and leadership. Managers, who have these attributes, have the necessary ingredients to move up through the Model. They also can produce good financial results. Furthermore a leader in the Empowerment Level who is strong in these attributes will create explosive competitive, compounding and financial value.

1.   *Desire*—The easiest way to test desire is to work inward. Desire feels like having something inside you that wants to get out but never really does. It's a drive or push for something. It constantly enters your heart and mind. It's like hunger; you have to feed it. Desire is created by unfulfilled needs and wants. Needs were explained in Chapter IV. Wants include specific items that fulfill needs such as cars, bigger homes, etc. The opposite of desire is complacency, apathy and laziness. If we're complacent about being introverted, we will not have the desire to learn how to work better with others. On the other hand if we have a great desire to work with people, we'll have also the necessary desire to improve our interpersonal skills.

2.   *Determination* is what happens when desire is amplified to a higher degree. The desire becomes so strong that we are unwilling to quit and we'll accomplish the goal no matter the personal cost or sacrifice. Olympic athletes are a great example of this principle. These athletes did not make it to the Olympics merely by chance or by expressing some desire; they made it to the Olympics because their relentless effort to become the best, no matter what obstacles they encounter along the way in their quest. That same type of determination will drive good managers to become effective leaders by making the sacrifice in time and energy to enhance themselves and to develop others.

3.   *Initiative and Discipline—Initiative* is the result of desire and determination. It is the action part of the two. There are five levels of initiative that really determine future progress in the Leadership Model as exemplified below from the lowest (1) to the highest (5):

1) Wait until told

2) Ask what to do

3) Recommend and then take decided action

4) Act but advise at once

5) Act on your own and report frequently

Good managers who are low on the Leadership Model tend to range between 1 and 2 on their initiative level. Leaders initiate at levels 4 and 5. These upper levels are necessary because they allow the leader to carry out the most significant aspects of leadership like creating an empowered atmosphere, implementation of new ideas, creativity, and vision. These aspects will not occur without a willingness and ability to act.

Closely tied to initiative is *Self-discipline*. This is the hardest thing we will do in our lives. When we enter self-discipline we deal with mastering our body, our thoughts, and our passions.

For our bodies we need to learn self-control so that we can master important body functions like sleep, which robs so many people of the stuff life is made of: *time*. These are all things that control us and to master our thoughts means to learn how to focus. We need to focus our thoughts on those things that help us be better people and anything else amounts to a waste of precious "human hard drive space".

Passions also need to be mastered and kept in check because too often certain passions can control our body and mind. Learning to control our body, thoughts and passions is the training ground for discipline. Building discipline is like building anything else in life; we can't take short cuts and we have to pay the price. Focusing on these three fundamentals will strengthen us sufficiently to tackle the other attributes of the Leadership Model.

Control Level

4.   *Planning*—Good management and leadership starts with planning as previously explained in Part I. Planning is used throughout the Leadership Model and is a function of control because planning is an incipient stage that allows controlling in most part the future outcome. It's also a function of leadership because planning determines in advance how to influence people.

5.   *Organizing* is the process of creating a controlled environment so people can work more efficiently and effectively; it is more than just maintaining a filling system. It includes task and project management in an efficient way so that there is a maximum value returned for the time invested. Organizing also means determining the team members' optimum work flow, by organizing each process in a flow chart. The flow chart visually displays the order of steps they need to take to complete the process in the most efficient manner. The flow chart

also assists in the design of jobs and specifies job duties beyond the normal day-to-day operational responsibilities.

6.   *System and Process Development* is the result of planning and organizing and is essential to effective management and for creating customer confidence, but unfortunately it is also the most neglected. Many managers never get to this point on the Model's scale because it appears much easier to wring it.

7.   *Measurement* is what needs to be done after creating a good process which is being followed. Measurement is the "seeing-eye dog" of control so to speak, because it helps to know exactly where you are.

8.   *Accountability* is a manager's greatest tool for control. Accountability confers the aspect of control for the people involved in the work process. People who feel accountable will act accountable.

There are two forms of accountability:

❖ natural accountability and

❖ direct accountability

Both are needed for different circumstances. Leadership blunders occur when natural accountability is neglected and direct accountability is misused or it is used as a threat system.

Natural accountability is creating a forum for individuals to report on their areas of responsibility and is the best form of accountability because it relies and nourishes upon the integrity and dependability of the individual team member. It is also an opportunity to use the Peak Performance Flowchart depicted in Chapter V. By providing natural forms of accountability management communicates to the team that the task or responsibility is important and worthwhile. If the individual has integrity and is dependable, natural accountability creates motivation to fulfill the responsibility without a continuous check ups from the supervisor or foreperson.

Leaders fail when they think (either consciously or unconsciously) that natural accountability is not needed when there's dependability and integrity. Of course that with dependability and integrity the job gets done but without natural accountability these qualities will soon run out of fuel. Frequently and constantly reporting on one's responsibilities, acts as a measuring yardstick for performance. Individuals who fail to report on anything meaningful or make excuses for not performing are showing a trend that indicates how their operations are being run.

In such cases where natural accountability fails to motivate performance, *direct accountability* is needed. It provides a change in mechanism. It calls for meeting with each poor performing person individually, directly confronting the individuals on the issue and provide an appropriate consequence. Direct accountability is about change in behavior and it is the leader's responsibility to first try to change the individuals by building them, training them and support them. If the individuals refuse to change, it is then the leader's responsibility to ultimately make a change by removing them from the position and replace them with appropriate personnel.

Direct accountability should always be conducted *individually* as in personal interviews or performance reviews. As leaders we also need to make our expectations clear, but there is a right way and a wrong way to do it. Here is where the most leadership blunders occur for many people with authority would jump right on and chop left and right because they only understand the "*direct confronting*" aspect of direct accountability. Because the objective is to restore the operation to peak performance, direct confronting the issue requires skill. It needs to be addressed through building, confronting and rebuilding stages. The degree and the purpose that they are used depends of course of the level of offense and the number of occurrences but a leader should spend, if at all possible, most of the direct accountability time in building the individual. The confronting method would then take a back seat to the building and rebuilding methods. The *Confront Method* clearly defines the problem encountered.

The last step in direct accountability is to provide an *appropriate consequence* and it is an essential ingredient to changing the situation. The consequence is designed to do one of two things: change the person's behavior or change the person altogether. There should be no other purpose or result in direct accountability; anything else falls into the category of negligence, threat and criticism which do not restore the operation back to peak performance.

A good way to handle this situation is to design a consequence that helps the individual remedy the situation and subsequently if there's no change or improvement then the person should be replaced. Multiple chances and multiple threats should be avoided because they are executed with a management (not a leadership) perspective—quick and efficient—but they waste time and money because they never induce change, they only induce repetition of undesired performance.

The Action and Control Levels on the Leadership Model are the basic functions of excellent management and provide a solid foundation for leadership. Their focus is on efficiency, cost effectiveness and driving financial results. In fact, most people stay within the boundaries of these two levels and never contemplate going beyond, because the results achieved here seem to be good. It is the management perspective: short and efficient. Nevertheless, issues that are related to people are not resolved, because the management perspective does not have a suitable answer for issues that take long time or encompass people-related matters. The next levels form the Leadership Perspective and provide answers to resolve all these problems.

Personal Level—build and prepare yourself

Personal level involves self-development and self-building, providing access to the incipient stage of a leadership perspective. The focus here shifts to being as *effective* as possible.

To become a great leader requires moving up in the Leadership Model and accomplishing that necessitates sacrifice; it takes a true principle of leadership to do so and it may be a sacrifice in salary to take a position with a lot of potential; or it may be giving up old habits, comfortable work behaviors, or thoughts. It may involve removing people who are in leadership positions but still struggle with level one issues despite the best efforts invested to build them. Or it may be sacrificing time, energy and resources to self train and self develop.

Progressing through the Model requires greater discipline, skill, time and commitment and is founded on the natural law of sacrifice (Chapter IV).

9.   *Self-evaluation* and the use of creativity and self-will to change—this includes evaluating current behaviors to see what consequences they are creating. This evaluation may also include the evaluation of team members, operations and sometimes even customers. Self-evaluation is critical; without it we continue to do the same things we have always done and therefore we'll get the approximative same results. To be effective, self-evaluation needs to be accompanied by change to the better. Change always begins from inside out; very rarely it is the other way around. Evaluation is the foundation for progress and it is a form of analysis. That helps us know where we should focus our creativity and self-will. Evaluation is like a microscope; it opens the door to viewing and under-

standing a world that is invisible to the naked eye. It opens the door to understanding ineffectiveness and inefficiencies.

Evaluation is the planning and organizing side of leadership. It's the time when we sit down, think out and plan the best strategy, resources and priorities for the operation. It is the time when we organize the team's roles as to get maximum involvement and commitment. Once we have self-evaluated to determine what our ineffective behaviors are, we are then ready to move to the next level of the Leadership Model.

10.   *Building character* through principles and virtues—is one of the main building blocks for developing yourself as a truly effective leader. Benjamin Franklin was proof that if you master certain principles you can become anything you choose, regardless of circumstances. This is the power of change and this is how change occurs. It's an incredible achievement to master yourself—to identify an enduring principle and then to incorporate it into your own character. It is unfortunate that so few attempt this; but for those few who do, success is their constant companion.

11.   *Learn and develop competencies* is another important attribute of a leader. A true leader is never content with the status quo and is in continuous search for knowledge and constantly develops competencies. New ideas and new skills are essential for competitive value and form the lifeblood of an organization. Leaders will seek out new experiences that will expand their capacity and skills.

This is accomplished by formulating a personal development plan which should include:

✓ A learning outline
✓ Balance

✓ Daily development in an interruption—free environment.

A learning outline describes the areas you want to increase the competencies in, as pinpointed by the self-evaluation process. Adding balance will provide the capacity to sharpen every aspect of your life and it may provide a development outline. One way to help remain balanced is to develop a personal balanced scorecard that contains physical, mental, social and moral quadrants.

❖ Physical Quadrant focuses on strengthening the body on the idea that a healthy body refreshes the mind.

❖ Mental Quadrant stresses the importance of increasing knowledge and mental faculties. For example, reading books on leadership or other stimulating literature will spur ideas and bring value to self-development.

❖ Social Quadrant deals with practicing inter-personal skills by engaging in social activities. This helps individuals to relate to others better and increase their influence or their leadership skills.

❖ Moral Quadrant exercises focus on enhancing individual moral compass through learning true principles or by getting involved in services with a high moral content (as is the military or in some cases religious services). Stephen R. Covey recommends one hour a day to sharpen your saw. Within that hour he suggests engaging in activities from each of these four quadrants (*19). The amount of sacrifice you put into your personal development will determine your aptitude as a leader. If you don't push it here, you'll not be very confident at the next level of the Leadership Model.

12. *Learn How to Influence, Motivate and Inspire Others.* As a leader the number one ability is the power of influence.

Minimally, there are three kinds of power: the power to reward, the power to coerce, and the power to order. These are the recurrent two currencies of the military and of many organizations that follow chain of command. The problem especially with coercion and fear is that they cannot be internalized (they are contrary to fulfilling any core need). They require constant monitoring and reinforcement. The "drill sergeant" remains in attendance as a permanent fixture. The third currency might be the obedience or lack thereof. Nevertheless, this third one is really a subtler version of the first two. Obedience or disobedience usually is followed by some form of reward and/or punishment.

Influence is generally given short shrift. Often it is subsumed or absorbed into power. Here, in fact, is a standard text book definition: *"Power is the force you use to make things happen in an intended way. Whereas influence is what you have when you exercise power, and is expressed by others' behavioral response to your exercise of power."*(*20) In other words, power is the cause and the influence is effect. But the issue has become more complex because of the two-way corporate feedback. The dominant form of downward communication has increasingly been supplemented by upward communication. Thus, it is now necessary to talk of power exercised downward as well as upward within the organization.

Typically, power exercised downward uses the traditional forms of coercion and fear, whereas upward communication stresses accepting or acknowledging authority. Although the amount of research on the two-way traffic of corporate communication is limited, what we know centers on perceptions of what determines success or failure, in either direction.

Some of the skills that will help influence and motivate people are expressed below:

- ❖ *Never Criticize, Condemn or Complain*—These three "Cs" are an easy trap to fall into and as human beings we naturally gravitate towards the easy and convenient paths; however, a leader will realize that people will never be influenced, motivated or inspired if these three Cs are a regular part of the work environment and the treatment they receive.

❖ *Call Attention to People's Mistakes Indirectly*—and by doing so the resentment is minimized and their defense mechanisms that stifle and snuff out their ability to exercise self-awareness is bypassed. With their defenses down, people are more willing to realize their own mistakes.

❖ *Praise the Slightest Improvement*—this needs to be part of your character to be used consistently, and it means that you need to become a person who naturally notices improved performance and then you need to be a person who acknowledges the improvement. For this to work you need to be sincerely happy for that slightest of improvements.

❖ *Make the Fault Seem Easy to Correct.* If you decide that you need to talk to a person directly, a good way to begin rebuilding that individual's confidence to perform is to make the problem seem easy to correct, By doing so you've thrown that person a rope and helped climb out of own emotional pitfall.

❖ *Give the Other Person a Good Reputation to Live Up To.* This falls into the category of Self-Fulfillment Prophecy explained in Chapter V. It establishes a subconscious challenge in that person's mind by helping the individual feel important, which becomes the driver for improved performance.

❖ *Talk About Own Mistakes before Addressing Others'.* When the core needs of others are violated, there's an emotional response derived from that which clouds the mind, confuses judgment and stunts all potential for improvement

(Part III). By talking of own mistakes prior to addressing others' shows that you are also liable of making mistakes and you can relate to the person at fault.

❖ *Begin Disciplinary Action with Praise and Honest Appreciation.* The easy way to correct performance problems is to be emotional, direct, blunt or even abrupt or to use the fear of removal power inherited with the management position. It's easy because it does not require any skill; all it takes is lose control. But is definitely wrong. The problem with this approach is that it causes the individual to lose confidence and the resentment growing inside may prevent the person from self-evaluating and thus closing the door to change.

❖ *Address Performance Problems by Beginning with Praise and Appreciation.* Instead of blowing up or forcing own authority upon others a skilled leader will channel own frustration towards creating a win-win situation. If a situation presents itself in which a performance problem needs to be discussed one-on-one, a good approach would be to come up with a list of good traits that will first build that person up. If the person continues to require discipline, then it may not be appropriate to begin with praise and appreciation; it depends upon the situation.

❖ *Bring Up an Eager Want in Others.* The key to do this is to shape your objective in such a way that will fulfill a need in others and they'll do what is required not because they fear retribution but *because they want to*.

Interpersonal Level—build and prepare others.

This level requires a great deal of self-confidence and its purpose is to help individuals feel confident as leaders to build others and prepare them for greatness. The very act of building up others helps build up the builder. Here again the power of compounding value presents itself.

But if the individual did not pay the price required to self-build there will inevitably be conflicts associated with building up others. The conflict may be related to adherence to principles and double-mindedness and deceit may take hold. Without character an individual may falsely seek self-enhancement through abuse of formal power and authority, or by bragging, or by withholding information so that it gives a spurious sense of self-importance.

Or, the conflicts may also be related to knowledge. An individual in a leadership position may feel incompetent around team members that may know more about something than the leader. This in turn may cause the individual to put his team members down for fear of being labeled incompetent in that respect; and that only when the person in lead has not built self on a foundation of principles.

13. Building Up Others in Your Communication. A leader needs to have the necessary skills to influence, motivate and inspire the teammates. As the leader follows the *formula for growth* (Part I) to fuse these skills into own character at the Personal Level, s/he will be able to naturally draw upon every skill to make communication with all the team members encouraging and motivating.

14. Commit Others to a Common Purpose. This is probably the most important leadership attribute in terms of getting the most of your team. First we deal with two components:

- ❖ Commitment
- ❖ Purpose

A leader must first create a purpose and then to commit others to it.

Purpose varies according to the situation; however, one constant remains that human beings need a purpose for doing things.

Viktor Frankl demonstrates very eloquently this need for a purpose when he relates his experiences as a clinical psychologist and as a prisoner in a Nazi concentration camp during World War II. Said Frankl: *"What man actually needs is not a tensionless state but rather the striving and struggling for some goal worthy of him. What he needs is not the discharge of tension at any cost, but the call of a potential meaning waiting to be fulfilled by him."* (*21) He found that the prisoners who survived the horrors of the Holocaust did so because they held fast onto a purpose in their life.

When a leader provides this purpose and gets everyone focused in on it, the results obtained by the group or organization are so much powerful. Regardless of their position or job description, people react positively when they feel that their job is important and when they are brought into the greater purpose.

This sense of purpose can be achieved at any level. Here's an example of a great world leader, Winston Churchill, giving purpose to the British people during perhaps the Great Britain's finest hour of the World War II:

"We have before us an ordeal of the most grievous kind. We have before us many, many long months of struggle and of suffering.

"You ask, what is our 'We' policy? I will say; "It is to wage war, by sea, land and air, with all our might and with all the strength that God can give us: to wage war against a monstrous tyranny, never surpassed in the dark lamentable catalogue of human crime. That is our policy.

"You ask, what is our aim? I can answer with one word: Victory—victory at all costs, victory in spite of all terror, victory however long and hard the road may be; for without victory there is no survival".

It was delivered at a speech to the House of Commons on May 13, 1940, in his first address as the newly appointed Prime Minister of Great Britain. However, in the business world the common purpose is not as easy to commit to as it is to commit someone to surviving.

An effective way for leaders to commit others to new company initiatives or to a common purpose is to subject them to The Commitment Wheel, an imaginary wheel that goes: Prepare > Commit > Follow-Up, Prepare > Commit > Follow-Up, and so on.

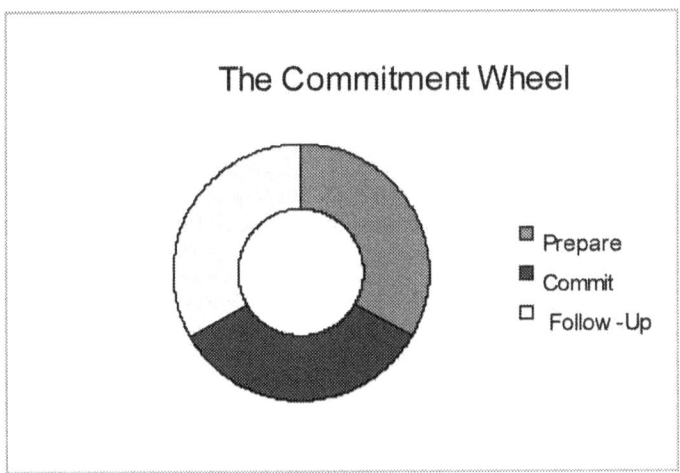

The *Prepare* component can be broken down into three parts:

1) Build a relationship of trust with the person

2) Enable that person to see and understand the vision

3) Help the person see own role in achieving the vision

Building a relationship of trust is the single most important factor for building a highly productive and cohesive team. People must first trust and believe in their leader before they will follow (commit to) their leadership.

Creating trust, respect and commitment are all the results of building yourself in the Personal Level. When you offer yourself as an example and behave in line with your principle-centered life you will naturally create trust in other people. Your native or learned interpersonal skills that were practiced to perfection will help you naturally treat others with respect. Trust must be upheld in every aspect of our relations with others. As a leader it is your responsibility to eliminate the backbiting and gossip, the two wrecking balls that will ultimately destroy any team. Otherwise the team will never reach its maximum capacity because the backbiting and gossip will destroy the very competitive and compound value a leader is seeking to achieve.

As a leader your goal is always directed towards establishing progressive, principle-centered teams where a person feels safe; a place where the absent person is always defended rather than attacked. This way the team will open up and allow you to build the team members because the trust factor simulates them to correctly respond to your team enhancement efforts. Trust needs to be established continuously, day by day. The key here is consistency. Building trust is essential. Taking the necessary time to teach vision and to help the individuals see their own role in the vision are the two other essential parts of preparing people for commitment. There are many ways to do that and numerous authors published works detailing these methods. In short, the best way to do this is the one that yields the greatest sense of importance. You are dealing with people here who require a leadership perspective; therefore, you need to be *effective*.

After you prepare someone for commitment, the next step is to personally *commit* the person with statements like "Will you…" which carries a built-in accountability. This statement *needs* to be followed up with accountability.

Finally, The Commitment Wheel requires *follow-up*. If a leader fails to follow up regularly with the vision or with the purpose that s/he commits others to, the leader is communicating that the vision or purpose is not important and does not really matter. Translated into human behavior it means that the vision will be forgotten and the purpose lost, being surpassed by things that are more urgent.

15.   *Follow Up Frequently With Those You Lead.* Leadership deals with constant and consistent feedback and follow-up. The team members need two forms of consistent and frequent feedback:

- ❖ Encouragement from being told that they are performing well. It is an unfulfilled core human need, and if we fail to do it we will violate their need allowing dissatisfaction to fill the void. However, if we provide sincere and frequent encouragement, the positive behavior will be repeated.

- ❖ The need to know as soon as possible when they are not doing well.

- ❖ Encouragement and feedback can be given in many ways and below are listed but a few:

- ❖ Praise the person around teammates.

- ❖ Take time to meet with the person individually and give praise.

- ❖ Write a note expressing your appreciation.

- ❖ Give the person a special reward (certificate, plaque, pin, etc.).

People also need to know when they are not doing well. When we fail to inform people of areas where they need to improve we fail to help them grow. It's impossible to build other people without this kind of feedback.

Follow-up is a process of being in contact with your people; it's an essential part of building up others. Regardless of how independent and effective people are, they still need follow-up; it is a way to communicate that you care as a leader. The follow-up is different with each person; if the task is critical, you should follow-up more frequently.

Follow-up is a form of communication; therefore, it contains everything, from the meaning of the spoken words to non-verbal communication, to value-added service. Everything we do during the follow-up communicates something about us. Leaders understand this and use it to their advantage. By being visible to our team members and to the customers through regular follow-up visits, we communicate that we care and that we're on top of things. Lack of follow-up communicates the opposite.

16. *Create a learning environment with those you lead.*

According to the natural law of growth, improvement can only occur through constant and continual learning; it's the only way and as a builder of others is the leader's job to provide it. One way to create a learning environment is to help the team members come up with a personal development plan. A good start in making a development plan is to assess where everyone is on the Leadership Model scale and then target each individual's weaknesses by developing specific action plans for improvement.

When assisting the team members in a personal plan, a good idea is to build-in natural accountability.

17. *Assess Leadership Capabilities of Those Around You.* An excellent leader knows the strengths and weaknesses of the

team members. That knowledge is needed so that the leader can begin working on building up and preparing the team members.

Empowerment Level—promote vision and inspire others to greatness.

This level is the fruit of trustworthiness earned at Personal Level and trust nurtured at the Interpersonal Level. In the Empowerment Level you empower trustworthy individuals so that they can reach their fullest potential. This is the art behind leadership and it's also where the greatest value is derived from. Management focuses on managing processes and systems while leadership focuses on extracting the maximum value from people and this is how an organization gets competitive, compounding and explosive financial value.

Leading at the Empowerment Level is the same as a farmer who assures that his crops grow in high-nutrient soil. The objective is to provide a perfect environment where the team members can grow and the perfect growth environment for human beings is a place that allows them to exercise their superior ability to act, to extend their talents, to take initiative and to be responsible for their growth.

For this to happen an environment founded on free agency must be established because dictatorial or hierarchical laden environments rarely produce people who reach their fullest potential. Human beings who nurtured in an environment founded on empowerment have unlimited capacity to produce unlimited results.

Many companies proudly state that their greatest asset is their people but only those who establish an environment that is founded on free agency and empowerment really prove that they believe in their statement.

18.   Create Team Structure

Having a team full of people sporting a leadership perspective is a guarantee that everyone within the team is executing the required plays with a pursuit of excellence. The principle of execution means everything for the team that strives to win.

Below is a succinct description of a way that teams could be structured for optimum performance in the service industry:

❖ Team paradigm shift and lingo adoption. By making a paradigm shift we switch our thinking into team thinking. As leaders we model team behavior, languages and attitudes which will make it easier for the team members to change their paradigms also.

❖ Team roles are probably a leader's greatest tool to empower and build his people. Roles provide opportunity for exposure to leadership and present a meaningful challenge where people can feel a great sense of purpose and accomplishment in their jobs. Roles are powerful when assigned to people using a leadership perspective. Some roles within a team may be Safety Mentor, Quality Assurance Specialist, Supply and Equipment Coordinator, etc.

❖ Team Guidelines bring order to a team and because the team itself is responsible for deciding what those guidelines are, everyone buys into them. Once everyone agrees to follow them the guidelines become the "rules of engagement"; they tell the team members how they should act in different situations.

❖ Team purpose, name and mission statement. Creating the team's purpose is essential to the team and to the leadership; it creates unity. Instead of only one person working towards the vision, everyone is committed to it. The commitment part evolves from each member's involvement in creating the team purpose and which is expressed in a team name and a team mission statement.

❖ Team meetings. This is where a leader has the opportunity to use the Peak Performance Flowchart (Chapter V); to meet core human needs (like praising and encouraging); to create natural accountability or to allow reporting on team roles assignments. This is a way to provide consistency in leadership and team meetings can be used to execute just about every leadership attribute on the Model scale.

❖ Standardized operating systems. Much like a computer, a company needs to have an operating system that organizes and controls all of the activities that occur. A team is no different—it needs to employ standardized operating systems so that the expectations are the same across the board, eliminating guesswork or uncertainty. Using these systems is proof of high professionalism and industry know-how.

19. *Create an atmosphere that empowers others to greatness and promotes vision.* As a leader you have to walk, talk and breathe empowerment. This usually takes a major paradigm shift. Most managers are accustomed to being the "go to" person for answers. They have been responsible for making the decisions for so long.

However, if you continue to always solve the problems and provide the answers yourself, you will fail in your leadership objective to build others and empower them and will destroy the competitive and compounding value that you can bring to the company.

The way to avoid this trap is to ask the team members who come to you for answers what they think that it should be done. By doing so you help them being decisive and you'll be surprised how capable and competent they are at solving the problems or providing the right answer—this builds their self-confidence, their creativity and their problem-solving skills. If you see that they are way off-course, make suggestions but refrain from the temptation of providing the answer yourself; just offer guidance.

By taking this approach not only will you be building people and nurturing their self-esteem, you'll be removing many monkeys from your back because you are no longer the only person who makes decisions. In addition you'll be creating the very foundation for empowerment atmosphere. This powerful practice, if executed properly will help your people open up, generate ideas and take ownership of those ideas. That is commitment. That is compounding value.

To create this empowerment atmosphere you need to talk the talk and walk the walk, meaning that you need to always refer to your people as team members or associates; you have to adopt the full language of the empowered environment. Leaders esteem their people to such degree that they will put them above themselves. For example instead of saying that Tom works *for me* you can say that Tom works *with me, he is part of the team.*

20.   *Creating opportunities for team members to advance.* Even after a leader has built a learning environment by creating and expecting continuous learning and even after a leader has involved team members in key roles on the team a leader still searches for and provides opportunities for people to grow and advance. These opportunities might include sending people to trade shows, or it might be including them in such activities as attending important meetings, bid walks or inclusion in special projects teams. It might include an opportunity to serve on a company cross-functional team or even

moving the person into a new position. As leaders we need to be prepared to let those who we mentor grow and go. There are numerous opportunities for your team members out there; it's your responsibility to sniff them out.

Level V Leadership

This is the ultimate level of leadership; is the pinnacle of any great leader. Level V leaders will channel their ego needs away from themselves and into the larger goal of building a great company. It's not that a level V leader has no ego or self-interest. Indeed they are extremely ambitious but their ambition is first and foremost for the organization and not for themselves (*3).

Level V leadership refers to the highest level in the hierarchy of executive capabilities and goes against the conventional wisdom that calls for towering personalities to build great companies or to achieve the breakthrough.

Think of Abraham Lincoln, whom Jim Collins names as one of the few Level V presidents of the United States. He never let his ego interfere with his primary goal of a much larger cause—creating a great and enduring nation. But those who took President Lincoln's personal modesty as a sign of weakness were terribly mistaken and the history is proof of that.

21.   *Build enduring greatness through a paradoxical mix of personal humility and professional will.* Level V leaders take the empowerment environment and the build-up of others to the next level by setting up their successors for even greater success in the next generation. In a contrasting comparison, great leaders who did not reach Level V often set up their successors for failure, subconsciously (or in some cases deliberately) feeding their ego by knowing that after they're gone, the whole edifice they created would ultimately crumble.

Level V leaders display a very workmanlike diligence and attribute their successes to factors other than themselves; they always attribute their organizations' achievements to the team. In contrast, every team member will admit that the achievements are nothing but the result of a great leadership and that all of them are just mesmerized by the character and behavior of their (level V) leader.

However, when something does not go well the Level V leader will immediately take full responsibility. This contradicts the natural tendency of human beings to take personal credit for accomplishments and to blame others for failures.

Potential Level V leaders are all around us if we take the time to look in the right place and if only we know what to look for.

Nobody can mentor us in becoming Level V leaders; this is where individual grit and resolve determines the outcome. Level V leaders are not greater-than-life personalities who are easy to spot and so we may have a hard time finding a model to follow in order to achieve Level V. The secret is in observing the astounding results that the organizations, under Level V leadership are able to consistently and repeatedly produce.

CHAPTER VII

CREATING EXCELLENCE AND RECURRING SUCCESS

"You were born to win; but to be a winner, you must plan to win, prepare to win, and expect to win".
Zig Ziglar, American Sales Trainer Author and Motivational Speaker

EXCELLENCE

What is Excellence? The word means to be superior to someone or outstanding in something. Excellence is relative to one's situation and the surroundings. For example, a high school quarterback might be the best in his league but put in different surroundings (such as the National Football League) he might be totally incapable. This example shows that standards vary according to one's situation. Higher standards are formed when a person achieves a new goal never obtained before or when someone learns something new. A person's skills, attitudes and knowledge determine that individual's standard. Therefore, standards vary greatly depending upon each individual's level of knowledge, skills and attitude.

If a company sets its own standard of excellence, it translates in an atmosphere of competition only if the leaders and their teammates think that the standard is too low and consequently they together will go all-out to raise it. On the other hand it may lead to complacency and laziness if the leaders think that they're the best when in reality they are just the best of the worst. As the Roman philosopher Seneca put it "It's not good to be the best of the worst".

Variations in standards make it difficult for individuals and companies to determine the value they are to create. This also creates a difficulty to promise a certain level of performance in terms of price and quality of service. Having a standard to measure against can help service-oriented companies and individuals know what value and level of service is expected, in line with the industry expectations.

As mentioned prior in the text, the ancient Greece's philosopher Aristotle explained that "We are what we repeatedly do. Excellence is not an act but a habit" (*23). If we apply the first sentence of this quote to the day to day business activities we get an incredible insight. What do we repeatedly do to communicate and coordinate our business activities? What do we repeatedly do to manage performance, build and develop our own individual capabilities as well as our team members'? What do we repeatedly do to set up work environments where others can succeed and how do we repeatedly reward the best performers? These are all very good questions and the intention of Chapter VII of this text is to provide some lucrative answers so that we can repeatedly be excellent in all that we do.

Having a standard can help us know where we are, where those we lead are and what we need to do to become the cream of the best. General Electric, for example, determined that in order to make the transition from a good company to a great one you need to be either number one or number two in your industry or you need to exit it(*3).

So in order to become repeatedly good at our business activities we first need to look at what is needed to create the standard of excellence and achieve success that repeats itself many times over. A good place to start is to learn how premier companies achieve operational effectiveness, durable success and then target our own individual operation.

Premier companies are referred to as high-maturity companies. This brings to mind the analogy of high/low-maturity companies with adults/adolescents.

Generally speaking an adult is expected to be more dependable than an adolescent. Therefore, we depend on adults for results more so than we would with a teenager for example. This stereotype is silly but makes a point: some organizations, for the same reason are more dependable than others in delivering results. With low-maturity organizations you are not sure what kind of results you're going to get.

High-maturity companies have a few common attributes, although they are not limited to the ones delineated below:

1. A unique and clearly defined position in the market.
2. A fully developed and effective strategy to achieve higher than average profitability results and to be best competitors in their market position
3. Have all their business activities aligned to support and reinforce their strategy and at the same time to serve their position in the market.
4. Have made their basic work processes as their primary focus for management.

High-maturity companies are different from their competitors in a way that is valuable to the consumer. They also have achieved operational effectiveness because they focus on the six basic work processes. As a result, they can generate more competitive and compound value than their competition.

In addition to competitive value, high-maturity companies create compounding value as well when they make all of their activities consistent with, reinforcing of, and optimized for their particular (and unique) strategy.

Consistent = being in harmony; free from variation or contradiction.
Reinforce = to straighten by additional assistance, material or support.
Optimize = to make as perfect, effective or functional as possible.

High-maturity companies do not happen by chance; they occur because of deliberate actions, business knowledge and the talents of company leadership and personnel. High-maturity level and the resulting enduring and repeatable success cannot be achieved unless a company creates the necessary organizational structures, mindsets and cultural activities required to achieve this level. For example the best organizational structures create unity, teamwork, collaboration and cooperation between executives or between workgroups. This kind of structure is essential for implementing a unique strategy throughout the company.

However, low-maturity companies (more of them than anyone might think) have organizational structures resembling the Middle Ages' feudal system. This consists of a king and powerful lords who own significant amount of properties and who pay taxes to their king so that they can use his protection in case of foreign invaders.

In companies structured in a feudalistic way the executives represent the lords and the CEO or president is the king. In principle the executives "want to do what's best for the company but because of powerful forces brought on by different perspectives on the business, they end up acting like medieval lords seeking favors from their king. Aware of the conflicting interests of the other lords, they protect their own turf and avoid attacking anyone's sacred cows" (*24). Ultimately, this type of company structure prevents executives from working as a team to decide on a company strategy and to align all business activities to that strategy. The feudalistic structure is creating barriers for implementing new activities throughout the "kingdom". This feudal system is common and therefore, it is possible to have high-maturity companies that have low-maturity pockets, or low-maturity companies that contain some pockets of high-maturity.

Low-maturity companies often lack a clearly defined position, an effective strategy and a dedicated commitment to basic work processes. Low-maturity companies are also undisciplined to stick to these three things. Low-maturity companies typically have only sporadic success and their success is at random. Sometimes if they are the best of the worst, they repeat what worked in the past and as a result produce higher profits until a competitor raises the bar or forms a new position. Success is as relative as excellence is.

Some of the symptoms of a low-maturity organization are:

1. Inconsistency in performing business activities
2. Avoidance of or shifting the responsibility
3. Poor communication
4. Emotionally detached workforce with poor morale
5. Work overload
6. Unclear performance objectives or feedback
7. Frequent distraction in the work process
8. Lack of relevant knowledge or skill

One of the main reasons that the symptoms enumerated above occur is because low-maturity companies lack focus on the six basic work processes. For example looking at staffing, low-maturity companies operate on the philosophy that any person can properly hire and obtain positive results. Poor staffing capability leads to hiring of company personnel who are typically unskilled and ill prepared.

With standards largely undefined, it is left to the individual managers to use whatever talents and abilities they have to carry out essential management practices. Furthermore, with undefined staffing processes, low-maturity companies are disabled in their capabilities to match the right skills, knowledge and abilities to the right people, leading to the hiring of the wrong people altogether.

In most low-maturity companies the prevailing assumption is that managerial skills come naturally to almost everyone or that by observing other seasoned managers, the less skilled managers can learn fast. There's some truth in this concept but most of the time managerial skills need to be developed. This leads to the necessity for learning the correct six basic work processes practices.

Since low-maturity companies rarely clarify the responsibilities of managers, inconsistence is to be expected. How people will be treated becomes a game of hit and miss, as managers rely on their own interpersonal skills and prior experiences in dealing with people which might not be adequate at all.

Managers in low-maturity companies lack a consistent vision of what the manager's fundamental responsibilities are, mostly due to misunderstanding of management versus leadership, as explained in Chapter VI. Or they might lack the knowledge or skill required to improve the performance of their team members. Training sessions are vague and ambiguous, often leaving the team members to design, develop and deliver processes themselves without the necessary skill and knowledge to do so, under a false pretense of empowerment.

Many people in low-maturity companies are promoted based on tenure, nepotism or past success. These companies do not realize or simply ignore the fact that there is considerable difference in the required skill and knowledge in the new position in comparison to the one held prior. Previous skills and accomplishments may indicate a capacity for creating new success but there is no total guarantee for future performance.

How do low-maturity companies, with such a perceived high level of incompetence still survive? The truth is that there is a huge number of low-maturity companies out there but because of the principle of natural selection in the business climate, the ones still surviving are doing a lot of things right and some are even successful, being more prevalent that one might expect.

The reason for that is the relativeness nature of success and excellence. If the consumer for example is used to and accepts mediocre service, someone a tad above mediocrity might appear as excellent or successful until a competitor pops up and shows what true excellence is by raising the standard.

In the comparison between high and low-maturity companies, it is not the point to show that low-maturity companies can't be successful or that they are a miserable failure. In their own relative surroundings many of the low-maturity companies are well regarded and respected. The point is rather to talk about the opportunity cost incurred by being a low-maturity company versus high-maturity; it's what you could have compared to what you're getting now.

High-maturity companies don't want to be out-performed and they are not satisfied with a mediocre to good status; they seek value maximization. This does not imply that high-maturity companies are perfect; they have problems and setbacks as well. However, these high-maturity companies have assured that infrastructures are in place to support all six basic work processes activities.

"Take my assets, but leave my organization and in five years I'll have it all back!" exclaimed Alfred P. Sloan, Jr. the late chairman of General Motors Corporation (*25).

High-maturity companies emphasize heavily that managers make the six basic work processes their highest priority.

THE SIX BASIC WORK PROCESSES

All the high-maturity organizations have a common denominator: they create repeating success as a direct result of focusing on and effectively using six basic groups of activities referred to as *the six basic work processes*. Research revealed that there are six components that are always required to achieve repeating success in any endeavor, namely:

❖ Staffing

❖ Communication and Coordination

❖ Work Environment

❖ Compensation and Reward

❖ Training and Development

❖ Performance Management

Turning the attention toward the understanding each of the six basic work processes creates the basis of achieving managerial success. It brings incredible power and clarification to management by showing what they need to succeed. When the going gets tough and an operation becomes problematic, the six basic work processes serve as a guiding light in troubleshooting and eliminating the negative occurrences, helping negotiate the rough waters and dire straits of redemption.

By analyzing the six basic work processes, management can quickly pinpoint which one has been neglected; this ability to break down activities is a powerful troubleshooting and analyzing tool for any operation. The scrutiny starts with the staffing process, which represents one end of the "durable success" spectrum. By breaking down a department or area that flounders, corporate management is able to see if the local team has the best staffing activities in place and if through their current practices the local management team is capable of obtaining 90% or better in hiring the best person for the job. Furthermore, the corporate management can determine if the local team spends the right amount of time hiring the right candidates, if they have the necessary skills to hire effectively, and if there is in place the required knowledge and expertise for training and retention.

However, the task of analyzing an operation is far from done. Next, the examination calls for a hard look at the team's performance management process, which represents the other end of the durable success spectrum. Sure enough, the hard look will determine if the local management knows exactly how their team is performing, beyond just the bottom line. It will show what activities are performed to ensure repeating success. It will reveal if there is accountability and consistent feedback, and if the goals are set according to the S. M. A. R. T. S. methodology. The analysis will also reveal if there are written and recorded consequences that will occur if the goals are obtained and if the goals are not obtained.

Third, the corporate management needs to evaluate the communication and coordination process, to find out if the local management has activities in place to consistently communicate value, and if the right activities are in place to coordinate the team's efforts consistently towards the best possible outcome.

Fourth, they need to examine the basic work environment process, to see if there's true motivation among team members, if there's true camaraderie and collaboration, and if there's unity and high sense of professionalism. If the outlook of the group is positive and optimistic, then the scrutiny continues deeper, to see if there's any emotional or physical harm in the work environment, if the job processes were identified, and if the corresponding job descriptions are in place.

The fifth basic work process that needs to be examined next is the compensation and reward, to determine if the employees are equitably paid for their contribution, and if there is a fair job evaluation plus a market evaluation process in place to assess the compensation level. The examiners need to determine if the recognition activities are consistently being carried out throughout the analyzed unit. The answer will clarify if the unit's people are holding back their best because they feel inadequately compensated and acknowledged for their work.

The sixth and last step in breaking down and analyzing an underachieving business unit is looking at the basic work process of training and development. Does the unit's leadership possess the knowledge, ability and skill required for successfully performing in each of the unit's positions? Are the training and development activities clearly defined? Are they consistently applied throughout the unit? What's the relationship between the training processes and the required job activities or behaviors? All these answers will provide the remaining puzzle pieces to create a complete picture of the unit at hand. After all the pieces fall into place, the solution for improving performance appears clear and concise. Whether used by a CEO of a major player in the economy or by entry-level managers, the six basic work processes represent the most important management activities. Fundamentally, the understanding of the six basic work processes proved to be the key to success for all prominent CEOs of our time. These remarkable personalities consistently dedicate an important amount of time to assure they have powerful basic work processes infrastructures in place and the necessary resources to support their business objectives.

STAFFING PROCESS

The staffing process represents the activities with the greatest possibility to affect performance and achieve enduring success. No other process has a greater effect or can change the outcome quicker than a fundamental change in the search, acquisition, and treatment of human talent. This process hardens all the other business activities, for talented and motivated people make the difference between average and stellar operations. To understand the importance of the staffing process, management needs to look at the flow of talent through their organization. There are three conditions that inevitably apply to any organization regarding how talent flows in and out. (*36) They are:

❖ Both positive and negative talent will certainly enter and exit an organization

❖ Undoubtedly, here will definitely be errors within the hiring process, allowing for some people to be mistakenly hired for a position within the organization

❖ Some good performers will inexorably become poor performers

These rules are highly intuitive and because of this, most mature companies and some of the low-maturity ones have some form of hiring process to control the talent flow. Research shows that, despite the general perception of human resources personnel being fairly good at the hiring process, most selection systems used at this time have a performance yield of no better than 40% to 50%. (*36) Performance yield is a concept established in manufacturing, but it can be applied to all processes responsible for accepting input and generating output. This concept depicts the percentage of the product (output) that will work as intended.

In most cases, the poor selection results were not the effect of bad hiring decisions as much as they were the outcome of a system which could not produce any better. This means that 50% to 60% of the new hires will not or could not perform as predicted, due to lack of specific skills, knowledge or attitudes required to achieve success. It adversely impacts an organization, to the point of almost crippling it unless there's an *intervening factor.* The accumulation of negative talent taking place in low-maturity organizations may not be that obvious, especially if the organization is the best of the worst in its market segment. It may even appear as if nothing is wrong, because some low-maturity organizations excel in their relative surroundings and conditions. However, what is less obvious is the difference in performance and in results between what was achieved and what could have been achieved had their positive talent collection been greater than the negative talent collection.

Leaders of premier, high-maturity companies know that the success of their firm is ultimately dictated by their ability to effectively manage their talent collection. These leaders have mastered the essential leverage methods in managing the talent flow and they have uncompromisingly engineered intervening processes to regulate this flow. In fact, they placed the talent flow management into a dedicated system intended to maximize positive talent attraction and minimize negative influences.

Intervening factors represent a series of processes designed to influence the outcome of the talent flow management. Some of these factors are:

❖ The recruiting and selection process. To attract new and positive talent into an organization requires skill and sustained effort; bringing in good talent doesn't happen by chance—it's a choice. Premier companies developed intense recruiting and selecting systems that predict an outstanding 90% or higher performance yield.

❖ The system implemented by the high-maturity companies for developing and improving the performance of the negative talent, for performance management, and for training and development. Typically, these premier companies allocate up to 4% of their whole payroll for training and development; in their quest to transform "B" and "C" employees into category "A".

❖ The method of dealing with underperformance. Leading high-maturity companies employ powerful coaching practices and performance review processes to intentionally target underachievers, using an uncompromising but at the same time respectful approach.

❖ The process introduced as a countermeasure for the time when top performing talent starts to become negative talent because of frustration, discouragement or negative management. In this situation, positive talent decides to inhibit performance or to display negative behavior to deal with their emotions.

❖ A management procedure to deal with the inevitability of a part of positive talent exiting the organization. For this situation, prominent companies design forceful compensation and reward methodologies with aggressive talent review to insure that all positive talent is accounted for, and an atmosphere where the top performers are encouraged to stretch their goals and step outside the box.

❖ Retention programs, representing the totality of activities that leading high-maturity companies deploy to keep their talented people. They become more flexible in their job description details, allow for creative environments such as telecommuting or virtual workgroups, they create upward mobility and challenging positions.

The staffing work process is outfitted with several activities which assist with the talent flow management in identifying and placement of the best person for the position. However, the requirements of this work process extend beyond recruiting, selecting and placing. It takes a powerful mindset for staying the course and not allowing the processes to be compromised when the pressure for immediately filling the vacant positions occurs. Sacrificing due diligence, using hastiness and "warm-body" hiring technique creates nothing but a vicious cycle of problems. The key is having and using a *talent frame of mind*; it requires a relentless pursuit and uncompromising determination to guarantee that each position is filled with the most talented individual available. A talent frame of mind calls also for an adamant tenacity to deal effectively with underachievers.

Attracting the right talent assures that the persons hired possess the necessary competencies, such as personal qualities, skills, knowledge and attitudes necessary to be a top gun. When the right combination of competencies is lacking, long-lasting success is hampered, because individuals can't see beyond their current situation. The individuals lack the ability to take themselves or their jobs to the next level, resulting in low morale, diminished initiative and dissatisfaction. These are not bad people by any means, they just need to develop the necessary competency level or find a place where their competency level is adequate, allowing them to succeed.

In addition to the talent frame of mind, the staffing process requires a *competency frame of mind*. This calls for identifying the existence or the non-existence of crucial competencies as the main provider to success or failure. Successful managers manifest most of the competencies listed below.

Personal	Inter-personal	Managerial	Technical	Intellectual	Leadership
Integrity	Customer focus	Goal setting	Job specific skills	Creativity	Inspiring others
Initiative	Verbal communication	Organization skills	General technical skills	Superior Judgement	Empowerment
Excellence	Non-verbal communication	Planning skills	Other general skills	Good decision making skills	Negotiation skills
Work ethic	Likability	Prioritizing capabilities	Computer usage	Intelligence	Vision
Energy	Listening	Performance management	Mathematics	Pragmatism	Team building
Tenacity	First impression	Talent mindset	Language skills	Analytical skills	Conflict management
Self-awareness	Team player	Diversity	Typing	Critical thinking	Coaching skills
Enthusiasm	Persuasion	Financial performance		Conceptual skills	Mentoring skills
Adaptability	Political Savvy	Human resources skills		Experience	Motivating abilities
Independence		Operational management		Systematic approach	
Assertiveness		Marketing skills		Education	
Stress management				Risk taking	
Ambition				Being on the leading edge	

A competency profile identifies all the required competencies needed for a particular job position. If a position requires, for example six major job duties, all the competencies identified as required for that job need to be measured for each of these six duties. The job competency analysis takes some time to complete but it will show exactly what it takes to be successful in that job position. It will lead to making fewer mistakes in the hiring process; it will provide a benchmark to measure performance and will show how to improve people. Also it will allow much easier to achieve the standard of excellence and outstanding results when the person screened matches the required competency levels.

Competencies require a written description of how the behavior within each competency is manifested, so that a hiring manager is able to compare and do an educated inquiry to determine whether individuals actually possess the competencies. This requirement confers a new image to the recruiting and selection process. Advertising then becomes more appealing to candidates who possess the targeted competencies. The interviewing process becomes also geared towards discovering if there's a pattern of the competency profile throughout a candidate's career, offering up to 90% accuracy in predicting if a candidate has what it takes to perform successfully.

Intellectual Competencies Profile

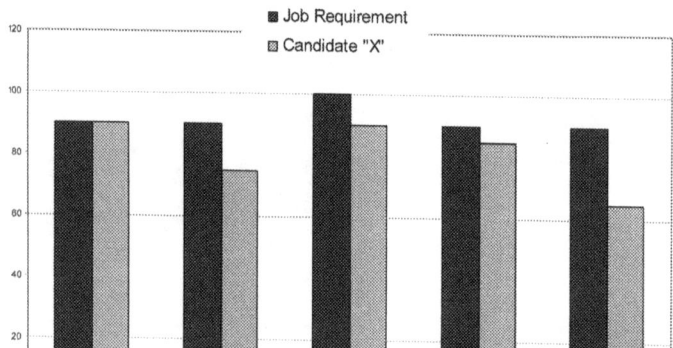

Can these competencies be improved or learned if the person is lacking? The answer varies depending upon the competency. Some are changeable with due diligence and hard work. Others, like Intelligence, Creativity, Integrity, Assertiveness and Analytical Skills are deeply ingrained in someone's character and seem to be intrinsic. These skills can be faked, but the counterfeiting is easily spotted and it is rarely sustainable. The performance management work process provides further answers to the question of possibility to improve and acquire competencies.

PERFORMANCE MANAGEMENT PROCESS

The performance management work process represents a group of activities that have the greatest potential to maintain the highest level of performance and quality throughout the organization. These activities create and communicate the high expectations set forth for performance and for improvement; provide support through effective coaching; and establish action plans with real consequences. This way it is enough accountability to assure an enduring success and to eliminate complacency and mediocrity.

While the staffing work process acts as the front entrance for attracting talent, the performance management process constitutes the internal engine for retaining the talent once inside the organization. It sets this process at the other end of the business process spectrum, making it as important as the staffing.

Performance management process allows the company leadership to determine how to use the remaining four basic work processes to support and reinforce the success created by their talented people. It also provides the necessary accountability and delineates clearly the expectations for the execution of company's business activities. Furthermore, the performance management activities are orchestrated in such a fashion as to assist company leadership in keeping track of the company's talent, in appropriately rewarding the talent, and in assuring that the most talented personnel continue to work at the highest level of performance.

Just as the staffing work process calls for a talent frame of mind, so also does the performance management work process. Here this mindset serves a different purpose—to require from management the relentless pursuit and unyielding determination to maintain high standards of performance.

A talent frame of mind in performance management calls for an effective method of dealing with underperformance. Managers need to have the emotional courage to decisively deal with underperformers. Failing to put the right people in the right jobs, and failing to fix people problems timely when they appear will ultimately make an enterprise flounder.

Performance management process can be viewed in a two-dimensional perspective: *individual* and *company-wide*. The individual dimension communicates management performance as helping individuals learn what their own individual competency level is in relation to the job requirements by assessing strengths, weaknesses, and opportunities. The company-wide dimension establishes an infrastructure to help the company leadership assess and keep track of the top-talented performers. All in all project management attains robust success by constantly cycling of the following activities:

❖ *Clarifying expectations.* Expectations start with a vision, which can be a standard of performance, a cultural perspective, or a marketing position. Good leaders extract from their vision all the drive necessary to enunciate and mold their expectations. The gap between the vision and the actual reality creates the force necessary to shape an expectation. That's how one can tell if a leader has a vision; because it will be manifested frequently and repeatedly during formal or informal dialogue, business meetings or marketing presentations. The ability to clearly express expectations shares the same S. M. A. R. T. S. characteristics as writing an effective goal.

❖ *Monitoring and observing results.* Subsequent to defining expectations, good leaders with a strong performance management mind frame will display a sincere interest in knowing how the individuals are performing. This requires frequent interaction and inquiry, without falling into the trap of micro-management. Performance management oriented leaders make themselves aware of the behaviors, actions, and results of their people, so that all these can be compared with the expectations, resulting in effective feedback. Leaders must be willing to listen and share opinions, observe performance and build rapport with the team.

❖ *Giving frequent feedback.* It should be a natural result of monitoring and observing, and it should correspond directly with these activities. With every inquiry it should be a candid feedback. Effective leaders also elicit feedback about their own performance, and what the leader can do to help the individual succeed. During the feedback session, leaders actually coach the individual, creating an environment where people feel open to sharing their thoughts and feelings about their performance. Every leader is expected to use coaching effectively to fulfill the action plans designed and set forth.

❖ *Action plans.* In effective performance management work processes, every feedback session concludes with an action plan. Each action plan details what actions the individuals will undertake, what are the leaders' actions and what's the time frame.

At corporate level, performance management expands upon the individual performance management cycle, thus giving a good understanding of what talent the company has to work with to achieve its business objectives. Corporate also needs to establish benchmarks against which unit and individual performance can be measured, reviewed and compared for improved results. It also serves to supply the necessary input needed by the training and development process and by the compensation and reward process. At the corporate level, the performance management cycle includes:

❖ *Company-wide talent review.* Prominent companies with strong performance management activities encompass some type of company-wide talent review process. This process carries the same level of importance as the budget review process. Its purpose is to determine what kind of talent is incorporated in the company, and compares it to what is required to be successful in the intended market segment. It also serves to identify the high performers for rewards such as stock options and advancements. Furthermore, it assists leaders in knowing who the up-coming talent is and what needs to be done to get it into a ready-to-start mode.

The information generated is used to plan for succession in key positions. A part of the talent review process is setting S. M. A. R. T. S. goals, which gives real meaning to clear expectations and performance. Periodic evaluations, which are usually fogged up with subjectivity and time gaps, become highly objective. Because the essence of a goal is to achieve a future state, it also allows getting continual improvement and success. If a company incorporates a system similar to the Equilibrium Square concept discussed previously in the text, it should require managers to set goals within each of the four areas of responsibility.

Some companies even have company-wide, web-based goal-setting management systems, tied into the company's database. The goals then can be measured and compared in real time with data coming from the field or from various sources.

Corporate Performance Management Model

First quarter Goal setting	Second Quarter Goal achievement and performance improvement	Third Quarter	Fourth Quarter Talent evaluation

Platform: Job analysis	
Forms:	By-weekly task chart for major job duties. Annual review.
1)	Participation in goal setting using SMARTS procedure in areas:
	– Equilibrium Square—"Results" area
	– Competency improvement for level "A" achievement
2)	Goals are set for the fiscal year with checkpoints at end of each quarter.
3)	Task charts to be used for weekly work towards the goals.
4)	Goals are graphically displayed on the web-based chart
5)	Goals are accessible to CEO, management, individuals, and the Corporate Human Resources Department
6)	Web-based chart allows for a visual depiction of goal progress.
7)	Goals are converted into percentages based on the total number of them set at the beginning of the year.
8)	Executives and management meet to identify the A, B, and C level employees, and who is a chronic level C.
	– People are identifies
	– Executive action plans are set in terms of:
	> A level employees development
	> B and C level employees performance improvement
	> Chronic C level employees redeployment or removal
	– Action plans are followed up on at six month intervals

❖ *Action plans.* Corporate performance management also assures that action plans are carried out for under-performers, and company executives are expected to follow through with these plans. Consequently, action plans are a key part of individual as well as corporate performance management activities.

COMMUNICATION AND COORDINATION PROCESS

The communication and coordination process represents a group of activities with a major impact on the perception of a company's product or service. This work process contributes to the achievement of durable success by communicating and coordinating the company's business activities to external and internal customers alike. The end goal of the communication and coordination process is to act as the company's value delivery system. It helps all employees know how to deliver the company's value proposition and at the same time is allowing the customer to become highly aware of the value received.

Communication and coordination activities combat negative customer perception by explicitly conveying what all the start-up, in-process, and close-out activities are. Furthermore, this work process gives a sense of purpose to all of the technological activities which enable the sharing of data between the internal personnel and the end customer in a way that enhances decision making and effectiveness.

The purpose of the communication and coordination process is to establish a clear value delivery system and form an integrated infrastructure for communication and coordination of data, strategy, solutions, progress, defects, action plans, etc. Two concepts with a heavy influence on the communication and coordination process are *the value proposition and the value delivery system*. Marketing guru Philip Kotler defines the value proposition as *"a cluster of benefits/activities a company promises to deliver with the product or service"*. (*37) It is used to assist the customer evaluate the difference between the total value and the total cost of doing business with a particular company. The point here is to demonstrate a lower or comparable cost, but a higher perceived value than the competition, creating a market advantage.

The value delivery system describes all the activities a customer experiences in obtaining, using and discontinuing the usage of a product or service. (*37) It consists of:

> ❖ *Start-up activities*. These activities are required when a new account comes about and may include everything from staffing to ordering equipment and supplies, to conducting the first two weeks of service. While the start-up activities happen all at once, the communication and coordination activities occur to constantly support and reinforce the value proposition in the customer's mind, and to control the value delivery system so that the customer is put at ease.

❖ *In-process activities.* They encompass all the activities carried out to service an account. The in-process communication and coordination activities continue to reinforce and support the value proposition in the customer's mind, while controlling the execution of all operational activities to the extent of reassuring that the value delivery occurs as intended.

❖ *The close-out activities.* They occur when a contract is lost, cancelled, or a production facility is shut-down. The purpose of close-out activities, besides recuperating all possible resources and movable goods, is to leave a better impression that during the in-process activities. In this case, the close-out communication and coordination activities are very effective in reinforcing the value proposition so that there's an increased likelihood that the customer will experience regret with the newly contracted company. It may even lead to reacquiring of that contract.

The ultimate goal of the value proposition and the value delivery system is to shift the customer beyond positive customer satisfaction and into customer loyalty, which is a more desirable lifetime value. Loyal customers, above and beyond just satisfied customers, will spend more, tolerate more and spread more positive word of mouth.

There is another facet of solid communication and coordination process. It needs to be supported by a heavily integrated information system which feeds and automate important data and customer feedback. These systems include call centers, web infrastructures, chat windows which provide answers in real time. The communication and coordination process allows a company to differentiate from the competition and to transmit value in a unique approach, because perception is everything for success achievement.

WORK ENVIRONMENT PROCESS

This process represents a group of activities with a major impact on maintaining and enhancing an atmosphere where talented people can succeed. Its purpose is to establish the best environment for people rather to wait for it to evolve over time. In deliberately establishing the best work environment, the primary focus of the work environment activities is to eliminate costly inefficiencies, redundancies, and trial-and-error. The work environment process represents the highest level of the empowerment level (level 20: create an environment where others can succeed and advance). It consists of four components:

❖ *Working conditions that motivate people and make them feel good about their work.* Strong success requires special conditions that generate an environment where anyone is motivated and feels positive, where the core human needs are fulfilled and where there is an eager willingness to succeed. Other special conditions might include things such as teamwork, friendliness, cooperation, learning culture or openness. Concepts like scientific management and empowerment attempt to create the most effective work structure where people will naturally be enticed to work at their optimum level, generating the maximum potential for achievement of durable success.

❖ *Clearly established key process components that are easily repeatable.* People must know key procedures and they must be able to effortlessly and effectively repeat them each time is needed. For that matter, the procedures need to be in writing, as SOP (standard operating procedures); the employees must receive adequate training on these procedures and the management needs to oversee their effective implementation. Best procedures are nothing more that business practices that have been carefully engineered and proven on the job to produce the best results. These practices require that the "leading edge" competency to be discovered and used. A leading edge competent person always seeks new and better ways to do things and expects the teammates to do the same. This is how the best practices and better cost-effective solution germinate.

❖ *Tools and equipment optimized for the task.* Company personnel must have access to the right tools and equipment which is optimized for the job at hand. This requires a constant assessment of the market segment and a continuous knowledge of the best equipment utilized throughout the industry.

❖ *Physical safety, emotional considerations and legal compliance.* People must feel safe and protected from physical or emotional harm. There must be effective training in workplace safety; there must be effective training on harassment and other interpersonal skills, to stave off any form of emotional harm; there must be knowledge and training on employment law pertaining to the unit's activities.

Having an established work environment process offers managers a method of measurement of their ability to repeat their past success. Having identified all the components of the work environment process, managers know exactly what needs to be done to be effective in a particular assignment, and it gives an excellent benchmark for determining if the business unit creates operational effectiveness.

COMPENSATION AND REWARD PROCESS

The compensation and reward process represents a group of activities with a major motivational impact on the team's drive to achieve durable success. It includes the job evaluation process, which asserts the particular demands of different jobs within the company. The purpose of the job evaluation is to provide a basis for linking differences of pay rates to the differences in job requirements. It also allows the company to institute equitable compensation and reward structures designed to compensate people for their contribution. There are different types of pay structures, from the traditional structures to competency-based pay structures, to broad banding structures.

The rationale of the compensation and reward process is to recognize, institute and uphold activities which compensate and reward individuals based on the value of their contribution to the company's effort. *Compensation* constitutes the amount of money given a person in exchange for the work completed, and deals directly with matching the money paid with the work performed. It has somewhat little influence on the level of performance and behaviors within the job.

Compensation activities must be:

- ❖ Internally unbiased; all people need to be paid in proportion to the relative value of their jobs.

- ❖ Externally competitive; all people need to be paid in proportion to the market price for their jobs.

- ❖ Personally motivating to employees.

- ❖ Easy to administer by human resources staff. (*38)

Reward has to do with recognition of a particular behavior, and is based on attempts to influence behavior. The ability to recompense others with psychological rewards calls for a full load of personal security and self-worth. When people have a high sense of self-worth and personal security, they are willing to share with others, allowing at the same time enough stock for "rainy days" when negative behavior, such as pettiness, backbiting, betrayal or gossip start to draw out from this savings stock. By analyzing the meaning of *reward*, we can get a wider image of how we can create real business activities for the compensation and reward process. This broadened picture allows becoming more creative in coming up with truly rewarding and motivating activities.

For a compensation and reward process to be successful it needs to meet the following three basic rules:

1) The process activities need to be based on the principles of motivation, and should consist of an appropriate blend of motivators and pushes. Table 3 below presents a scale depicting the most encountered motivators and their gradient of satisfaction.

2) Reward activities must be consistent with and reinforcing of the activities that will create results. Do not just reward mere results. This rule follows the previous basic rule: in order to achieve maximum results, compensation and reward need to be connected to the activities and behaviors required to be successful, and to support and strengthen them. The most important thing a manager can do as a leader is to align the kind of rewards given out with the kind of behavior s/he desires to have in the organization. However, if the rewards are based solely on results, the activities which create those results remain unsupported. In this situation, the creation of durable success could be done ONLY IF these activities can be easily repeated. When compensation and reward activities are based only upon results, the course to achieving those results is often obscured, and becomes difficult to replicate and repeat.

3) Reward the best performers, not the worst. The talent frame of mind comes into play here, and many companies structure their compensation and

reward process towards recompensing the "A-level" employees the most, the "B-level" employees sometimes and the "C-level" employees the least, be it with stock options or other perks.

The compensation and reward process encourages the motivation necessary to achieve robust success, and it must be centered on a complete job evaluation conducted by qualified personnel.

Category of motivation	Type of motivation	Motivators encountered	Satisfaction gradient	Sustainability (low to high)
EXTERNAL MOTIVATORS	Physical abuse	Compliance or Resentment/Hatered	-10	
	Psychological abuse	Compliance or Resentment/Hatered	-8	
	Verbal abuse	Compliance or Resentment/Hatered	-7	
	Sarcasm or criticism	Compliance or Resentment	-6	
	Threatening body language (frowns, dirty looks, etc.)	Compliance or Resentment	-4	
	Non-violent threats	Compliance or Resentment	-2	
	Friendly and accommodating work environment	Neutral - this motivator is universally expected	0	
INTERNAL MOTIVATORS	Basic core human needs are met	Neither dissatisfied nor satisfied	0	
	Salary and fringe benefits	Internal recognition for worth	1	
	Other monetary compensation (bonus, comission, spiffs, etc.)	Internal recognition for worth	2	
	Award ceremonies	Internal and external recognition for worth	3	
	Removing some controls while retaining full accountability	Responsibility and personal achievement	4	
	Increasing accountability for personal work completed	Responsibility and recognition	5	
	Offering a complete and naturally delineated work unit	Achievement, responsibility and personal recognition	6	
	Granting additional authority	Achievement, responsibility and personal recognition	7	
	Job freedom	Achievement, responsibility and personal recognition	8	
	Making periodic reports available directly to employees	Internal recognition	9	
	Introducing new, more difficult or more interesting tasks	Growth and learning opportunity	9	
	Assigning specialized individuals or specific tasks	Responsibility, growth and achievement	10	
	Allowing employees to become experts in their field	Responsibility, growth and achievement	10	

Tab. 3 Motivator scale and gradient of satisfaction

TRAINING AND DEVELOPMENT PROCESS

This process encompasses all activities which assure that company personnel have the necessary competencies to fulfill their job duties to the highest level, and achieve success in carrying out corporate or local unit initiatives. Without the right competencies, an initiative will only go so far or it will run out of propellant. A solid training and developing process therefore requires a culture of continuous learning to be able to meet the challenges of the future. With a competencies paradigm, company leaders realize that for the most part, the necessary competencies do not always come or exist naturally—they must be acquired. This is the reason why prominent industry leaders have created corporate universities and spend 3% to 4% of their total annual revenue on the training and development process, while other organizations spend a fraction of 1%. It is futile to launch an initiative with the potential of creating competitive edge without first making sure that those involved in its implementation have the necessary competencies to do so.

In low-maturity companies, the training and development process is perceived as an expense, whereas in prominent high-maturity organizations it is considered a long-term investment which will yield results every time a new business activity is successfully carried out. It means that by constantly learning competencies through a carefully designed training and development program, people are able to bring value to their company. Achieving results from training requires a systematic method carried out by skilled professionals. It relies on some key activities which form a best practice system, referred to as the Instructional Process Design.

General Electric is one of the best companies in the world at identifying, sharing and executing best practices. General Electric has established what is known as a learning culture.

Robert Slater writes *"How does a learning culture work? In GE's case, it has adapted new product introduction techniques from Chrysler and Cannon; effective sourcing techniques from GM and Toyota; and quality initiatives from Motorola and Ford. Jack Welch [GE's CEO] is very proud that GE didn't invent the quality initiative—Motorola did, and Allied followed up with it; only then GE adapted it. It's a true badge of honor (…) to grab good ideas and run with them, regardless where they originate. There's nothing intrinsically wrong with that. Indeed, it's a virtue."* (*39)

Through their communication and coordination process, General Electric has learned how to identify and implement best practices. In fact, General Electric uses various tools to quickly adopt best practices and spread them throughout the organization. One such tool is called "The Best Practices Matrix", where the current business practices within the unit are compared against the new best practices the company has identified and wants to implement. (*39)

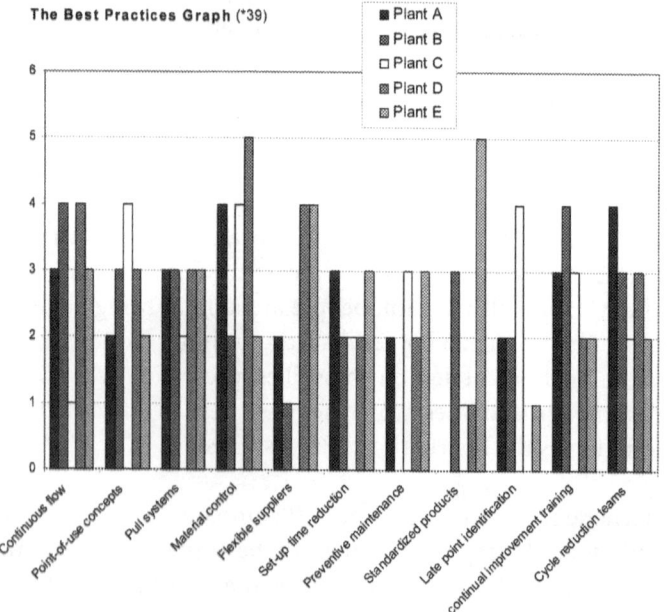

The Best Practices Graph (*39)

One of the major roles of the training and development process is to ensure that the company has the continual long-term capability and capacity to meet its business objectives, set forth by the company's strategy. When a company does not have the adequate capacity, it will respond to a new insight or to a new idea created at a higher level of thinking by involuntarily trampling it for not recognizing its benefits.

So, practically all prominent companies have dedicated significant resources to their training and development process in order to increase their capacity and capabilities. There are literally hundreds of corporate universities or academies formed for this purpose. One of the most famous is Crotonville, the General Electric's corporate university, known for its unique instructional strategies and for being a changing agent for the corporate culture.

Whatever the case might be, an effective training and development process requires dedicated leadership. The leadership will use this process as a direct intervention to make their initiatives victorious. Therefore, training and development is essential to creating and maintaining a company's competitive advantage.

ACTIVITY INTEGRATION

To avoid operating at a low-maturity level we must know to what extent to perform the six basic work processes activities. This calls for learning the definition, significance, and impact of our business activities. Then, we need to learn how to organize the activities so they operate at their maximum potential.

An activity can be a process, policy, practice, technology, or simply a choice, which can have minor or major consequences for the company. For example, a minor activity within facility services industry could be an inspection, whereas a major activity (common to all industries) could be the complex corporate activity of acquiring (purchase) of another company, relocating the business to another geographic region, or acquisition of major technology such as a data center.

Companies use hundreds of activities to design, develop, produce, sell, support, and deliver their goods or services to the consumer. These activities are categorized into two main groups, *primary activities and support activities.* Then, they are further grouped under departments as described in the Chapter I of this text.

PRIMARY ACTIVITIES

Primary activities deal directly with getting the product or service to the customer. They include:

- ❖ In-bound operation activities, which deal with getting the materials and labor necessary to create a product or perform a service.

- ❖ Operations (or Production) activities, which deal directly with the manufacture of a product or the performing of a service.

- ❖ Out-bound operation activities, which deal with delivering the product to the customer. In the building services industry this category of activities is non-existent.

- ❖ Marketing activities, which are primary activities that encompass the best mix of product, price, product promotion and market analysis for the proper positioning of the product to achieve the greatest possible returns using the company's value chain.

- ❖ Service activities, which are designed to support a customer's usage of a product and provide maintenance of that product.

Each primary activity is designed to produce revenue and enhance profitability within the company (*26).

SUPPORT ACTIVITIES

These activities, as the name implies support and strengthen the primary activities, so that the best product or service is provided. They add value to the chain by making the primary activities more efficient and effective. Support activities include:

* ❖ Accounting activities, which consist of accounting systems designed to identify, record and report the company's transactions

* ❖ Financial activities, which provide a methodology for obtaining the money needed by the company and then plan its usage. Financial activities confer added value to the company's value chain when they provide useful insight that enhances management's decision making capability.

* ❖ Human Resources activities, which are designed to assure that the best and most talented people are recruited, selected, hired, trained and retained.

* ❖ Technological activities, which are support activities that serve and augment the value chain by making the work easier and more productive. Technological activities confer access to information systems and integrate all the other activities so that repetitive or duplicate activities are eliminated.

* ❖ Purchasing activities, which provide support by assuring that all primary activities are supplied with the best resources at the best price. They add value to the chain by reducing the company's cost structure.

* ❖ Legal activities, which deal with the legal framework of all the activities and minimize liability. They may also seek justice in case of wrongdoing.

❖ Quality activities, which help measure and control the quality of the product or service provided and eliminate any waste, errors, and inefficiencies within the value chain.

❖ Cultural activities, which help create unity and oneness by promoting company's culture and eliminate unproductive atmospheres and mindsets.

In many businesses, support activities have not been formed to strengthen and support primary activities as much as they have evolved out of the necessity to fulfill legal requirements or to manage the basic functions of the business.

VALUE CHAIN

All primary and support activities work symbiotically together in the terms of the value they create for the company and the customer. Michael E. Porter, professor at Harvard University and strategy expert offers a model that describes how primary and support activities work together to form a value chain (*26). This simple model shows how activities are grouped within a company and how these activities directly influence profit margins. Porter calls the model *"the value chain"* because all the activities within a company are interlinked like a chain in the overall value the company can generate. The value chain describes the activities that directly influence the value a company can produce. Here is a simple and straightforward representation of Porter's value Chain Model:

	Inbound Operational Activities	Operational Activities	Outbound Operational Activities	Marketing and Sales Activities		Service Activities
PRIMARY ACTIVITIES	*~Work loading activities* *~System set-up activities* *~Supply distribution activities*	*~All the services performed and the activities associated with them*	*~Distribution* *~Delivery*	**Product** *~Variety* *~Quality* *~Design* *~Features* *~Brand* **Price** *~List Price* *~Discounts* *~Credit terms*	**Promotion** *~Sales* *~Advertising* *~Sales force* *~Public relations* *~Direct marketing* **Place** *Channels* *Coverage* *Location*	*~Repair and Maintenance* *~Customer Service*

SUPPORT ACTIVITIES	**FIRM INFRASTRUCTURE** Quality activities, Planning activities, Cultural activities, Accounting activities, Finance activities, Legal and Government activities
	Human Resources Activities Staffing activities, Payroll activities, Safety activities, Performance management activities, Compensation, recognition and reward activities, Training and development activities, benefits and employee relations activities
	TECHNOLOGY DEVELOPMENT ACTIVITIES Research and development activities, Information Technology activities, System design and development activities
	PROCUREMENT ACTIVITIES Supplies and equipment purchasing activities, vehicle purchasing activities, Deal negotiating activities, Cost analysis activities

Difference between Total Value and Total Cost — **PROFIT MARGIN**

It is important to notice how every activity, whether primary or support, influences the profit margin of the company. This is demonstrated by the horizontal rows that lead to the tip of the model, which is the profit margin. Also each primary activity is supported and reinforced by all of the support activities. The profit margin represents the difference between the total value generated by the primary and support activities and the total cost of these activities.

Going back to the high-maturity versus low-maturity companies dissertation, this model shows how detrimental it is to the overall value a company can generate if its activities are inconsistent; or if a company organized under a feudal system can't integrate its activities and can't make each of them consistent with and reinforcing of the company's position and corresponding strategy.

The value chain model demonstrates a large scale grouping of activities but it does not define exactly the specific activities that each company performs. It serves as a guide to help a company know what activities it must embark on to create value. The model shows also where the company should have specialized personnel performing the activities. Without these specialized professionals, companies lack the skills knowledge and attitudes required to obtain maximum value and higher bottom line profits.

This is the trap low-maturity companies find themselves into. Low-maturity companies think most of the time that the "one man show" philosophy can save operational or other costs if a manager does everything. Of course, costs can be saved by consolidating and having people do more—this is efficiency. Too often though, low-maturity companies lack specialized individuals and therefore find that their managers are trying to be experts in all things. The end result is mediocrity at best. These activities are often diluted, or short cuts exist, thus reducing the ability to generate maximum value and ultimately heftier bottom line.

The number of activities within a value chain depends upon what is needed to carry out the strategy, and what is the cost the company is willing to incur. Even though the model doesn't depict every activity that a company should have, it provides a place for every activity; therefore, when a company chooses its activities, it can organize each of them logically, according to whether the activity is of a primary or a support category.

In identifying, classifying and assigning activities, Porter's value chain model assists managers in understanding that every activity affects in some way the total value a company is capable of producing. It helps a company reflect upon adding or deleting an activity. After all the activities are identified, understood and categorized, they can be assigned to business units within the company's organizational scheme which have the appropriate skills, knowledge and attitudes to make them successful. This approach makes the company strategy easies to carry out.

Each company needs to make a choice of what activities it will perform. Low-maturity business thinking leads to the addition of activities without too much consideration on how well they will fit within the strategy. The type of activities the company performs should be controlled by the company's strategy. It mandates that the company needs to choose what strategy it will pursue. A company strategy depicts the way it has decided to compete within the industry that will ultimately lead to a competitive advantage. Furthermore, a strategy is the identification of a unique position within the market and a choice to dedicate resources to maximize the position.

A good example of a high-maturity company that fell into the trap of low-maturity thinking is Chrysler Corporation. In the first few years of Lee Iacocca's leadership, Chrysler emerged from near-bankruptcy to one of the greatest success stories of the 20th century business world. Five years of stellar performance in the early eighties, then decline into crisis again. *"Like so many patients with a heart condition we'd survived emergency surgery (…) to revert to our unhealthy lifestyle"* wrote an insider. (*27) Chrysler, during the mid-term of Lee Iacocca's tenure, diverted its attention from the strategy of becoming the best auto maker to immersing in the Italian sports car industry (by acquiring Maserati, a business fiasco; Maserati was purchased by Ferrari later). Then, as if this was not enough diversion, Chrysler decided to go into corporate jets business (Gulf Stream jets) and into the defense industry. Fortunately, Chrysler was revived a second time during its 1990s turnaround after Lee Iacocca's departure, but it eventually sold out to the German company Daimler-Benz, creating Daimler-Chrysler.

When all activities are determined by the company's strategy, these activities will be reinforcing the successful execution of the strategy, and they will be optimized for excellence. If a company lacks a clearly defined strategy, then there are inconsistent activities that are sometimes conflicting with each other. The company's personnel are likely to be confused as to what is the value that they are providing.

The real value of Porter's value chain model lies not within the model itself but within the processes that companies must go through to align their activities to their strategy. This process is called *activity integration*. It includes:

- ❖ Identifying the activities within the value chain
- ❖ Understanding, categorizing and assigning these activities
- ❖ Optimizing the activities and aligning them to reinforce the company's strategy

Activity integration is carried out by the company's leadership when they do strategic planning. This integration process helps managers know how to make their individual activities consistent with and reinforcing of the strategy.

The process activity integration provides several benefits to companies.

1) Because there are only a limited number of activities a company can perform, its leadership can easily identify where the value is coming from. To gain this benefit, company leaders must identify and define the activities within each value chain group according to what is needed to carry out the strategy, and in report to the cost the company is willing to incur. Furthermore, by keeping the number of activities limited to a well-defined few, the company avoids the confusion to what type of value it provides. Therefore, the company's personnel can become specialized on these few activities that the

company has chosen. Also, by separating and classifying activities into primary and support types, upper management knows exactly what area of expertise is required to develop, add, and manage new systems. As a result, the company knows exactly what activities to train on, to manage performance for, and which activities to recognize and reward for excellent results.

2) By identifying these activities and linking them to the company's strategy the integration process enables a company to better understand how to execute primary and support activities more efficiently and effectively than the competition. Superior integration confers a competitive advantage because the results are greater profits and a sustained ability to maintain that profitability.

3) The integration process improves the analysis of the value chain associated with other activities. Using the value chain, a company can identify the activities that the other competing companies perform for each grouping and can benchmark its own value chain, thus identifying its own strengths and weaknesses, the threats and the opportunities. Additionally, because many companies evolve in an ad-hoc manner they tend to become bureaucratic, resulting in slow and clumsy execution of business activities. By comparing the complete picture of activities of a company with the same thing of another competitor, an organization can pinpoint its own bureaucracies which prevent it from being lean and agile in the marketplace.

4) The usage of the value chain model in activity integration helps companies be different than their competitors. Managers can identify which activity adds differentiated value to the customer, and they can analyze the cost structure of the activity to assure that they are offering the greatest value for the lowest cost possible.

5) The integration of activities assists companies in figuring out how organizational structures and charts should be formed to support value within the chain, eliminating redundancies and inconsistency. The organizational chart communicates how responsibilities are divided up. How communication flows and how relationships interact between business units. The most functional and effective organizational charts are created based on how the structure can best support and execute the company's strategy and yield a higher value within the chain. However, many organizational charts are made for other reasons besides that of creating a structure for supporting its value chain and its corresponding strategy. For example, some charts are created from the need of dividing responsibilities and understanding how communication should flow. Sometimes the organizational charts are made up on the fly in an ad-hoc fashion, as business comes in. Operational units should instead be organized and should function in terms of how to add value to the business model.

6) It allows verifying whether the company's activities are fully integrated and reinforcing of each other. It allows also seeing if these activities are consistent with the company's strategy. This means that the activity integration process forces trade-offs. A trade-off means here that more of one activity necessitates less of another.

When activities are integrated, the value and power will be generated by the sum of all the activities working together and compounding each other. To the contrary, when companies try to provide value to the customer employing disjointed activities, there is inconsistency, minimum impact, and more often results in damaging one's own image. When activities are inconsistent, it takes more time, money, and effort to work with or rectify the damage created. This situation also leads to a thinner bottom line, because inconsistent activities sometimes cancel each other out. Activity inconsistency often occurs within the slow, unnoticed evolution of a company; therefore, it is difficult to recognize this inconsistency especially when the company's activities become more complex. Success or failure of a business unit or company is based on the mix of activities chosen. When all of the chosen primary and support activities are combined and consistent with each other powerful results can be obtained.

Southwest Airlines is a great example of integration of activities that are aligned with their strategy and of the elimination of everything else. Southwest Airlines has been the profit leader in the airline industry for the past twenty years, and is the only profitable airline of the top six. Their strategy was to compete against the automobile transportation in terms of speed and price. To do so they used a blend of specialized activities that was different than the competition.

- ✓ Southwest Airlines chose a standardized fleet of Boeing 737 aircraft which lowered the price of new acquisitions and maintenance. They provided a quick 15 minute turn around at the terminal by eliminating assigned seating and eliminating in-flight meals, thus reducing the fare price also.

- ✓ Southwest Airlines uses lean, motivated ground crews, supported by such incentives as attractive compensation (competitive wages and benefits), stock option, and profit sharing.

- ✓ Southwest Airlines chose not to perform costly activities such as baggage transfers and making connecting flights with other airlines. They also avoided large crowded airports and hubs, essentially eliminating all activities that proved to be inconsistent with their strategy. The fact that Southwest Airlines chose not to perform certain activities is a demonstration of clearly defined trade-offs. By making those trade-offs, Southwest Airlines was able to do more with less, to integrate its activities to form a low price, to reach an efficient cost structure that led to less turnaround and more flights (*32).

From a competitor's point of view, it is easy to copy an individual activity but it is nearly impossible to copy the tightly intertwined value chain, because of the complexity and the complicate organization of all its integrated activities. Cost is what prevents the competitors to copy a successful model as well. It would simply cost too much for a company to change its structure starting from scratch. Companies which achieved consistency and reinforcement of their activities became very difficult to compete against.

The power of the six basic work processes and the impact they have on the value chain would rightfully warrant a careful analysis of each individual process. This analysis though is beyond the scope of the present text.

Each individual basic work processes' uniqueness becomes evident when they are fully integrated, and when they are included in the launching of company initiatives. In addition, the uniqueness of these six basic work processes comes from the high level of dedicated effort and the resources that are created once their true significance is understood. When company leaders realize how powerful the six basic work processes are and how they simplify business they tend to allocate a considerable amount of energy in making these six basic work processes as effective and as unique as possible. On the other hand if the basic work processes are separated, company leaders and management would work with each process isolated. It would then lead to the individual process being lost in the value chain due to the tendency to consider one process as being more valuable than another.

Based on all the activities discussed so far, management can establish a platform for building and launching any strategic initiative. An example of such platform is depicted here. It includes all of the activity groupings within the value chain.

PLATFORM FOR STRATEGIC INITIATIVE

- ❖ PLANNING ACTIVITIES
- ❖ ACCOUNTING ACTIVITIES
- ❖ FINANCE ACTIVITIES
- ❖ QUALITY MANAGEMENT ACTIVITIES
- ❖ LEGAL ACTIVITIES
- ❖ PROCUREMENT ACTIVITIES
- ❖ HUMAN RESOURCES ACTIVITIES
- ❖ MARKETING ACTIVITIES
- ❖ TECHNOLOGICAL ACTIVITIES
- ❖ OPERATIONAL ACTIVITIES

1) STAFFING

1. Job Analysis
2. Recruitment system
3. Selection system
4. Placement system

2) COMMUNICATION & COORDINATION

Within the following:

1. at start-up
2. during the process
3. at closing

3) WORK ENVIRONMENT

1. Work environment design

2. Work & Service processes
3. Cultural re-enforcement
4. Tools & Equipment
5. Safety

4) COMPENSATION & REWARD

1. Job evaluation based on market
2. Performance based variable pay
3. Performance based bonus
4. System based recognition
5. System based incentive program

5) TRAINING & DEVELOPMENT

1. Learning boot camp
2. E-learning infrastructure
3. Talent development program
4. Instructional system design

6) PERFORMANCE MANAGEMENT

1. Talent review process
2. Goal setting
3. Action plans
4. Coaching and mentoring

This platform can also be used in troubleshooting problems incurred within a business unit. If a unit is struggling, the first step is to make sure all the six basic work processes are executed perfectly. If we found that all the six basic work processes are executed well, then the problem is in some other activity group. Once the problem is pinpointed, we can make adjustments or changes based on our findings.

With the understanding of the six basic work processes and their tremendous importance, the ground is prepared for understanding operational efficiency, looked at through the "optical prism" of the value chain. This being said, the platform for launching strategic initiatives becomes a monobloc as illustrated below.

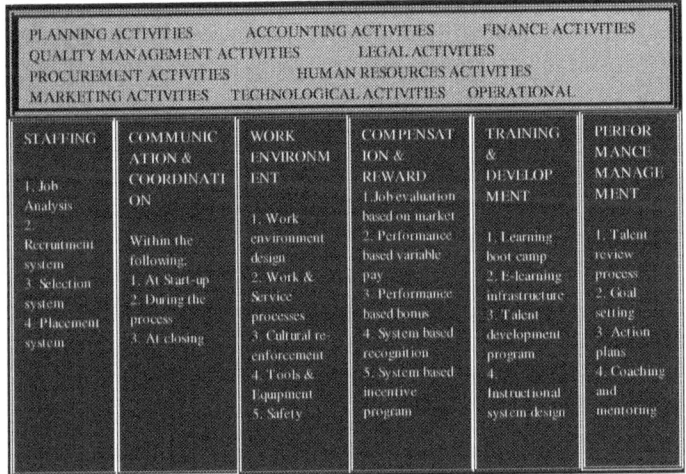

PLANNING ACTIVITIES   ACCOUNTING ACTIVITIES   FINANCE ACTIVITIES
QUALITY MANAGEMENT ACTIVITIES   LEGAL ACTIVITIES
PROCUREMENT ACTIVITIES   HUMAN RESOURCES ACTIVITIES
MARKETING ACTIVITIES   TECHNOLOGICAL ACTIVITIES   OPERATIONAL

STAFFING	COMMUNIC ATION & COORDINATI ON	WORK ENVIRONM ENT	COMPENSAT ION & REWARD	TRAINING & DEVELOP MENT	PERFOR MANCE MANAGE MENT
1. Job Analysis		1. Work environment design	1.Job evaluation based on market		
2. Recruitment system	Within the following:	2. Work & Service processes	2. Performance based variable pay	1. Learning boot camp	1. Talent review process
3. Selection system	1. At Start-up		3. Performance based bonus	2. E-learning infrastructure	2. Goal setting
4. Placement system	2. During the process	3. Cultural re-enforcement	4. System based recognition	3. Talent development program	3. Action plans
	3. At closing	4. Tools & Equipment	5. System based incentive program	4. Instructional system design	4. Coaching and mentoring
		5. Safety			

OPERATIONAL EFFICIENCY ACTIVITIES

Operational efficiency is different from operational effectiveness; sometimes it is a misnomer and sometimes it is misunderstood altogether.

Creating operational efficiency simply means to make activities within the value chain more efficient by minimizing their total cost. This is accomplished by shortening time allotted for a process or by eliminating unimportant or redundant steps. By doing so the process takes less time and repetition or overlapping is eliminated, demanding less resources, hence lower cost. If done properly and consciously, operational efficiency can have a big impact on the net profit a value chain creates.

Support activities should help make operational activities more efficient. For example quality is a support activity within the business' infrastructure. Quality activities include unique processes like *Overall Quality Management* or the *Six Sigma System*. This Six Sigma System is more aggressive than Overall Quality Model and is a disciplined method of eliminating nearly every defect from a company's activities. It projects focus on eliminating or improving operational activities that are considered to be costing the company more than they should. Using statistical methods, Six Sigma System seeks to decrease those costs. It teaches key six sigma and lean improvement principles, it provides a robust and comprehensive improvement model and trains people in the use of tools to achieve tangible results (*28).

Technological support activities are another example in this regard. Enterprise Resource Planning systems tie all of the company's value chain activities into one database so that repetitive, slow and labor intensive activities are consolidated or eliminated. Enterprise resource planning is a term derived from material resource planning. Enterprise Resource Planning systems typically handle the manufacturing, logistics, distribution, inventory, shipping, invoicing, and accounting for a company. Enterprise Resource Planning software can aid in the control of many business activities, like sales, delivery, billing, production, inventory management, and human resources management. Enterprise Resource Plannings are often called *back office systems* indicating that customers and the general public are not directly involved. This is contrasted with *front office systems* like customer relationship management systems that deal directly with the customer. Enterprise Resource Plannings are cross-functional and enterprise wide. All functional departments that are involved in operations or production are integrated in one system (*30). If done properly, the Enterprise Resource Planning makes company activities more efficient.

Support activities do not always make operational activities more efficient. This is true in companies that have lost sight of the value chain concept because as soon as the fact that every activity should add value is forgotten, bureaucratic thinking trickles in. Bureaucratic thinking means that there are support activities within the value chain which consider primary activities as their ancillary activities. Given all of the political, social and legal factors that impact a company, it is easy to see how companies could lose sight of the value chain concept and fall into this mode of thinking.

Consequently operational efficiency is about reducing waste, trimming the fat, eliminating redundancy and defects or increasing productivity throughout the value chain. However, any competitor can easily duplicate operational efficiency. Nonetheless, premier companies have one advantage when it comes to operational efficiency. The intricate and symbiotic relationship amid their six basic work processes activities creates a level of efficiency and a pattern of connectivity that is hard to duplicate. To do so their competitors would first have to figure out what the interrelation is—not an easy task because as mentioned prior, each of the competitor's six basic work processes traditionally has been buried within the value chain and works isolated from the others. For that reason duplication would require major changes in the competitors' processes so they would incur greater costs. They may not be willing to accept the rigors of greater costs or they may not be capable to sustain the added costs altogether.

STRATEGY

When a company's activities are said to be effective, it means that they support, reinforce and are optimized for the company's strategy—this is *operational effectiveness*. Business leaders are often distracted by the day-to-day decision making and by the constant changes in the socio-political and economical factors as sometimes they tend to lose sight of how to achieve operational effectiveness. This makes hard to focus on a particular strategy. Strategy is the creation of a unique and valuable position within the market place by deliberately allocating company's resources to achieve sustainable competitive advantage. The first part of this definition talks about creating a unique position. The concept of positioning means that a company has found a way to compete differently than others in the market, a way that customers are willing to pay for, often at a premium rate. The premium price comes from the fact that there are few, if any competitors to fulfill customers' need. So for a unique position to exist there must be three basic elements:

❖ *Needs that are unfulfilled*. It means that no company is meeting these needs; therefore, there's no competition.

❖ *Customer purchasing power*. Those customers that are being targeted have the monetary resources to pay for the value (of goods or services) brought by that unique position.

❖ *A unique offer*. It could be a product, a service, a price, a place or a promotion to fulfill that need.

The second part of the definition of strategy is about allocating company resources, which means dedicating things like cash, facilities, personnel, time and energy to serve the unique position (niche) that the company has created. Ultimately, competitive strategy is about being different; it means deliberately choosing a different set of activities to deliver a distinctive and inimitable value which will be more attractive to the consumer. If we consider the six basic work processes as the foundation of a well built edifice and the platform for strategic initiative as being the floor, we can deem that the columns and the roof could represent components of a sturdy strategy. This simplistic analogy is used here just to make a point: in a company strategy, the roof represents the company's strategic theme and the company's tag line.

The strategic theme is the refinement of the company's strategy into a clear, concise simple, memorable phrase that can be easily communicated throughout the organization. *"It should force trade-offs between competing sources and demands; [it should] test the strategic soundness of a particular action; and set clear boundaries within which employees must operate while granting them freedom to experiment within those constraints"* (*31). The result is the ability to have the entire company on the same page as to what value the company's personnel would create within the value chain. A strategic theme would also tell managers where they should invest resources. As mentioned before, General Electric's strategic theme is *"Be number one or number two in every industry in which we compete or get out"* (*31).

The tag line is nearly identical to the strategic theme but is used for a different purpose. It is the refinement of the company's strategy into a clear, simple, concise, memorable phrase that can be easily communicated to the consumer. GE's tag line for that matter is "We bring good things to life" (*31). It is clear that the strategic theme and the tag line are consistent with each other, they reinforce each other and they are optimized for each other. The more the strategic theme can serve to guide the management and at the same time to communicate to the consumer the company's value proposition, the more likely is that the strategic theme and the tag line will be similar.

In the aforementioned building analogy, the supporting walls represent the factors within the strategy the company decides to compete on.

SWA - Meet customers' short haul needs at low fares
The speed of a plane at the price of car travel

| LIMITED PASSENGER SERVICE | SHORT HAUL – SMALLER AIRPORTS | VERY LOW TICKET PRICE | HIGH AIRPORT UTILIZATION | LEAN / HIGH PRODUCTIVE GROUND CREW | FREQUENT AND RELIABLE DEPARTURES | FRIENDLY SERVICE | COMPANY TARGET: CAR TRAVELERS | STRATEGY |

PLANNING ACTIVITIES   ACCOUNTING ACTIVITIES   FINANCE
ACTIVITIES   QUALITY MANAGEMENT ACTIVITIES   LEGAL ACTIVITIES
PROCUREMENT ACTIVITIES   HUMAN RESOURCES ACTIVITIES
MARKETING ACTIVITIES   TECHNOLOGICAL ACTIVITIES
OPERATIONAL ACTIVITIES

STAFFING	COMMUNICATION & COORDINATION	WORK ENVIRONMENT	COMPENSATION & REWARD	TRAINING & DEVELOPMENT	PERFORMANCE MANAGEMENT
Job Analysis Recruitment system Selection system Placement system	Within the following: - At Start-up - During the process - At closing	Work environment design Work & Service processes Cultural reenforcement Tools & Equipment Safety	Job evaluation based on market Performance based variable pay Performance based bonus System based recognition System based incentive program	Learning boot camp E-learning infrastructure Talent development program Instructional system design	1. Talent review process 2. Goal setting 3. Action plans 4. Coaching and mentoring

OPERATIONAL EFFECTIVENESS

SOUTHWEST AIRLINES STRATEGY STRUCTURE

These factors form the company's points of differentiation. They represent the infrastructure of the strategy and they are designed specifically to be consistent with the company's strategic theme and tag line. Here is an exemplification of some of Southwest Airlines' points of differentiation which are consistent with and reinforcing of the roof (the strategic theme/tag line).

How is a strategy theme different from the mission statement? What's the purpose of the mission statement if there's a clearly stated strategic theme and a good tag line? The answer is that a mission statement drives a company's culture. A strategic theme drives a company's strategy. A mission statement is aspirational; it gives people something to strive for. A strategic theme is action oriented; it enables people to do something new. A mission statement is meant to inspire front line workers, whereas a strategic theme enables front line workers to act quickly giving them explicit guidance to make consistent choices (*31). The mission statement is what it is engraved on the front of the edifice.

The roof is supported firmly by the walls and pillars, which represent the points of differentiation. The strategic theme/tag line/mission statement (roof) and the points of differentiation (pillars/walls) form *the strategy*. These structural elements transmit the weight of the strategy to a solid platform for strategic initiative. The platform is in turn capable of sustaining and at the same time capable of transferring the bearing load to the six basic work processes which form a powerful foundation. The platform and the foundation represent *the operational effectiveness.*

Strategy is about being different in creating sustained competitive advantage. There are three generic strategies according to Michael E. Porter (*26).

❖   **Cost leadership** strategy strives for low cost production so that lower prices can result, separating the company from the competition. Typically there's only one cost leader within an industry. When others strive to compete, price wars engulf the profit margin and the bottom line. Cost leadership typically requires a value chain that has extremely low overhead, a plentiful resource of low cost labor force and efficient training and retaining systems that reduce or eliminate turnover. Cost leadership occurs usually when a company has a new cutting-edge technology, preferential access to suppliers or when they have an economy of scale (ability to purchase in huge quantities). Costco and Home Depot are examples of companies that chose the cost leadership strategy.

❖   **Differentiation strategy** seeks to be unique by performing the same activities as the competition but differently, or performing different activities altogether. This results in greater value to the chain and to the consumer. Differentiation comes in many shapes. Differentiation can be based on the marketing activities, for example. Or it can be based on the services provided, the way the service is performed, or the way the company networks. In contrast with cost leadership, there can be several differentiation strategy activities within one industry, as long as they are substantially different and generate sufficient value to attract customers willing to pay a premium price. Differentiators also seek to reduce costs but they do so in activities other that those which make up the differentiation part of the business. This allows them to stay competitive in price, yet to offer a significantly higher total value. In order to be meaningful and valuable to the customer, a differentiation needs to be:

- *Important*—The difference delivers a highly valued benefit to a sufficient number of consumers willing to buy.

- *Distinctive*—The difference is delivered in a distinctive way.

- *Superior*—The difference is superior to other ways of obtaining the benefit.

- *Preemptive*—Competition can't easily copy the difference.

- *Affordable*—The consumer can afford to pay for the difference.

- *Profitable*—It will be profitable to implement the difference.

If the differentiation fails one or more of these tests, it is unlikely to be successful (*33).

❖ **Focus strategy** (Cost focus and Differentiation focus) means self-positioning to serve a narrowly defined segment within the market (market niche). It allows for increased focus in better serving the needs within the segment. A market segment or niche represents a group of customers with a similar set of wants (*33). Even though a focus strategy does not create an overall competitive advantage, it does create a narrow competitive advantage because companies which deploy a focus strategy can optimize their resources in a way that better fulfills the few narrowly defined needs of the consumer. An example here is Jiffy Lube which provides a narrow but highly sought-after range of quick services for the vehicle owners, namely oil changes. Jiffy Lube achieved therefore a competitive advantage over the full service repair stations which also perform oil changes.

There are literally thousands of areas where companies can set up generic strategies. Every industry has numerous segments in which companies can decide to get involved. The most successful companies profile and concentrate their activities according to one of these generic strategies. When a company tries to perform activities for all three strategies, they are caught in the middle, by trying to be all the things to their customers. Typically companies in this situation struggle with profitability because they have so many activities that conflict with each other.

Looking again at the Southwest Airlines we observe that the company chose a focused-cost leadership strategy. Continental, in contrast, tried to differentiate itself from the other airlines by presenting a wide array of full service packages. Remarking Southwest Airlines' success, Continental decided to duplicate their strategy, yet they still tried to maintain their old full service package mentality. The outcome proved to be catastrophic. Continental found out that the focus-cost leadership strategy was inconsistent with its full service value chain. The result was a value chain with total cost exceeding its total value—the recipe for bankruptcy.

Smart and cautiously choreographed strategies consider the forces that interact within an industry. The most successful strategies indeed influence the competitive forces to the company's advantage. Understanding these forces can help leaders understand why some strategies are elected to the detriment of other ones.

Characteristically, profitability is perceived as a by-product of good managerial control. Besides this aspect, there are additional large-scale forces that have an even larger effect on a company's bottom line. These forces are often beyond a middle manager's control. Michael Porter has named them *"The Five Forces Model"*, represented herein. (*26) The model represents one way to describe how competition is formed. These five forces influence directly the industry's profitability and the participating company's profitability.

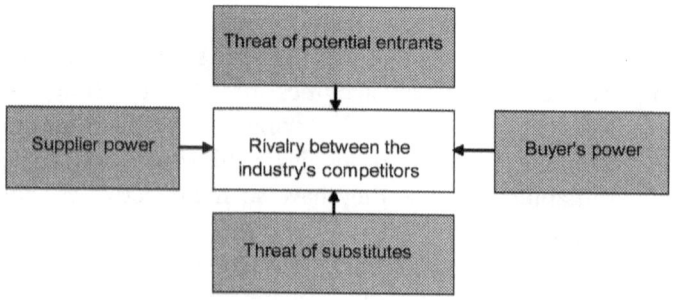

Due to this state of facts, a good strategy aims at identifying and performing activities which influence the five forces, resulting in improved profitability. Let's take a quick look at each of the five aforementioned forces to understand what lies behind a good strategic initiative.

Threat of intense competitor rivalry

When multiple competitors exist within an industry, their fierce antagonism creates price wars. The more intense the price war, the lower each company's profits become. Furthermore, high levels of competition means there are more choices for the consumer, strengthening therefore the buyer's power. The ideal situation is to find areas within the industry where the majority of the industry's competition can be successfully eliminated. This is where strategy helps. Invariably, part of the strategy should include a deliberate choice of what area of the industry a company is going to be involved in. In the Southwest Airlines example, they chose to serve small airports and shorter distance fares, targeting this way customers who, given a choice, would have traveled by car. This decision reduced the amount of competition in this particular market niche of the air travel industry, increasing at the same time the company's bottom line.

Threat of new entrants

The easier it is for new companies to enter an industry, the more competition it will foster. The same holds true for exiting companies: the harder it is for a company to exit a given industry, the more competitors will exist in that industry, drawing away potential customers from each other. If the companies are also poor performers, they create a negative perception about that particular industry. In such situations, the market as a whole or the market niche becomes less desirable.

Strategy should be aimed at making it difficult for new competitors to enter the market and make it easy for old competitors to exit. This strategy can be accomplished in various ways, some of which are mentioned here.

❖ A company can increase the amount of capital needed to penetrate a market segment. The greater the needed upstart capital, the less attractive it becomes for new competitors because the inherent greater risk that they will incur.

❖ An existing organization may be willing to increase the amount of learning and knowledge needed to successfully enter a market niche. Employing proprietary system designs and processes, an organization can make it very difficult for potential entrants to learn how to compete.

❖ By having the own value chain aligned with and reinforcing the strategy, and by employing sophisticated processes which are complicatedly intertwined, an organization creates its own unique model; making it very hard, if not impossible to be copied and duplicated by other competitors. So, even a much touted and talked about model in a particular industry does not represent alone a ticket to enter the industry.

❖ One way to make it easy for competitors to exit the market is through acquisitions, mergers and attractive buy-outs.

Threat of substitute products

A market niche or an industry becomes unattractive when there is a threat of substitute products. Soft drinks companies like Pepsi have been seeing clones or substitutes, such as juices or bottled ice teas, cutting in and eroding away its profits. Same holds true with the steel industry, which sees a stiff competition from substitute materials such as plastics, fiberglass, aluminum, or other alloys, which have displaced steel as a raw material for the finite product of many companies.

Strategy should be orchestrated and implemented to fend off the potential for substitutes. When developing strategic activities, the threat of substitutes must be taken into consideration and addressed to insure the continuance of the company's competitive edge.

Threat of buyer's power

When buyer power is high, it makes it difficult for suppliers to negotiate profitable pricing. Buyer power increases when buyers become more organized and more concentrated. It also increases when the product or service represents only a small fraction of the buyer's total expenses, when the price paid for the product or service is sensitive due to low margins of profit (tight market), or when the switching costs are low. Switching costs represent those incurred by a buyer when switching to a different supplier; the higher this cost, the more difficult and un-attractive it becomes to "jump ship".

Threat of supplier's power

Supplier power impacts industries that rely on major purchases for raw materials. If suppliers can effortlessly raise their prices or reduce the quantities supplied, then the supplier power is high. Suppliers tend to be powerful when they are concentrated or organized, when there are few substitutes or alternatives, and when the cost of switching is high. Also, when the demand is high and the supply low, supplier power could dictate the market trends.

Strategies should be developed to help reduce these forces. Every one of these five forces has a direct effect on the company's value chain. The value chain is the generating or the diminishing factor of the company's profit margin; that's why the five forces have a greater impact on profitability than the direct control measures instilled by the management.

However, they are both imperative and vital in maximizing the value within the chain.

To summarize, any change in the value chain will have a direct positive or negative effect on the company's profit margins. Each link in the chain is inseparably connected to an integrated network of activities where the old adage "you are only as strong as your weakest link" has grim consequences if an organization has not integrated its activities. The essence of strategy is to enhance the company's ability to earn and sustain healthy profits.

Managers may consider their jobs as being composed of carrying out the daily activities that assure coordination, performance and customer satisfaction. These are some of the primary responsibilities and definitely they are important. However, in the light of what we discussed above, managers have also two crucial responsibilities; both of which are designed to drastically affect the value that a company provides.

Primarily, the managers' responsibility is to make sure that the execution of the six basic work processes activities is as close to perfect as possible. The perfect execution will naturally bring about an enhanced ability to outperform the competition in providing the best service to the customer at the lowest price possible, and should never be compromised if managers truly aspire to be "A" players.

Secondly, managers are to assure that the strategic activities are executed with near perfection so that the customer will really feel the company's value chain and consequently will remain loyal. This also should never be compromised if a manager expects to be competitive and profitable.

The six basic work processes and the strategy define a manager's work, by providing purpose for professional and for personal activities. Strategy strengthens and enhances focus, allowing for proper resources allocation; it provides the reason behind strategic initiatives and alliances, lending greater support.

EPILOGUE

"Fit no stereotypes. Don't chase the latest management fads. The situation dictates which approach best accomplishes the team's mission".

Colin Powel, US Secretary of State, 2001–2005

Effective management and leadership are exercised over time across a wide array of responsibilities, across an entire business organization involving a variety of people who are accomplishing a multitude of tasks, concurrently of in sequence. The leadership must entice high performance and assure the well being of the whole group. Therefore, managers and ultimately savvy leaders can't consider their position and actions being a popularity contest. Trying not to offend anyone or trying to get everyone to like you will definitely set you on the road to mediocrity. That's because leaders who are afraid to rock the boat and upset people are likely to procrastinate and hesitate when it comes down to making tough decisions.

Leaders who are more concerned about own popularity rather than being effective are unlikely to confront the people who need a performance revival or an attitude adjustment.

Organizations, like people, get into ruts and as the business environment continually changes around them with the emergence of new technology, different demographics and a changed competition, these organizations tend to become archaic. This is a big problem and it is one of the reasons that more than half of the companies that appeared on the list of

Fortune 500 in 1980 no longer exist (*34). They could not adapt quick enough to the changing environment.

Managers need to be ever vigilant as to spot changing trends and to be quick on their feet and agile in adapting to the surrounding business climate. By employing the techniques described in this text, any manager can grow and advance through the Leadership Model and eventually achieving the hallmark of leadership, by becoming a Level V leader.

One of the leader's role as pointed out throughout this text is that of generating consensus as a result of healthy debates and empowered thinking, through which the members of the team are not afraid to challenge the status-quo. The leader always needs to be crystal clear of the general direction that the organization needs to be steered into, so that double-mindedness and ambiguity are eliminated. Therefore, the leader needs to be very methodical and deliberate in setting out the catalyst for change in the organization. A tremendous amount of time is required to be allocated for listening, learning, and involving people in the process.

Good managers and leaders focus relentlessly on making sure that their best performers are the most satisfied because ultimately it is people, not plans, systems or technologies, which make the difference between organizational success and failure.

Good performers develop the best ideas, generate the most creative action plans, and implement these plans better than anyone. Managers don't attract and retain these people by simply treating them like everyone else; they need to differentiate, by rewarding accordingly the top performers and at the same time refusing to pamper the mediocre. After all, your best people are those who support your agenda and who deliver the best results. Those people deserve and most often expect more; the rewards come in the form of additional compensation, but more often as accolades, career advancement, personal development opportunities, or assignment to premier projects. If they don't get what they deserve even the best performers become flat, de-motivated and cynical. Because they are aware of their marketability they'll start looking at other organizations for satisfiers.

That is why successful leaders like Jack Welch, CEO of General Electric or Steve Ballmer, CEO of Microsoft are adamant about three things: providing everyone with an opportunity, gratifying the best players with the greatest rewards and getting chronic underachievers off the boat.

Empowered working atmosphere is a beneficial factor in the advancement of managers to the goal of becoming great leaders. Many managers had already perceived a regressing trend in sticking with the status-quo, and are more willing to rewrite the rules. In all likelihood, far too few managers act on the perceived need for a change in the way things are. They either do not operate within empowered enough environments or are not sufficiently courageous to step outside of the boundaries of their own comfort zone, taking on unfamiliar and challenging new responsibilities. Or maybe they are afraid to upset people in their quest for changing things for the better, because they are hesitant in confronting employees, peers, or partners whose performance is under standard or no longer appropriate for the goals.

Using some of the skills learned in this text any manager can size the opportunity and act upon it benefiting their company and their own selves as well. Good leaders are breaking the pattern, continuously reshaping the mold when the innovations thrive. They continuously root out the barriers of communication and the flow of information both inward and outward. They understand the importance of rejecting the superficial evaluation, and delve into the underlying reality. They continue to probe deeper in search for discerning the truth from smoke.

As managers, the fact of "who we are" is packaged in "what we do". We carefully create what becomes the status quo, only to find ourselves trapped in it. Our self-esteem, enterprise infrastructures, cultures, and traditions along with our view of the competitors and customers make us who we are in the workplace. This is perfectly understandable because humans are creatures of habit, and habits serve us well, making us predictable and easier to work with.

The problem crops up when our habits dwell in the past. It is tempting to see the today's market as being pretty much the same as the marketplace of yesteryear, when we fought good battles and achieved success. Unfortunately it can't (and will never) be. Effective leaders consequently look beyond yesterday and today, and they don't cling to familiar territory; they ferret out clues to what tomorrow may look like. They plot a new course according to the perceived new information and constantly help themselves, as well as others to adjust to the circumstances as to better reflect the business climate of tomorrow (*34).

Many organizations out there trumpet the empowerment and using a common farming analogy they preach "pushing the water (read: *authority*) down (*the chain of command*) to the last row (*front-line employees*)". But looking beyond the rhetoric, seldom there is more empowerment in the new, non-traditional organizations than it is in traditional hierarchies with Byzantine bureaucracy. It may be a bit more freedom here and there, but this only pinpoints how much further the empowerment in these non-traditional organizations need to go to really loosen up, and before their people will take even modest risks for the benefit of the enterprise. Smart managers who feel prisoners of the aforementioned situation will try to push the envelope, to stretch things towards their limit without always asking for permission. They set their "S.M.A.R.T.S." goals—the last "S" in this acronym stands for *stretched*.

The mediocre manager will basically carry out standing orders and passively wait for new ones to come down the pipe. Sometimes they complain about the irrelevance or unfairness of the situation, but they still don't do anything to get out of the reactive zone and elevate themselves to the proactive environment. In contrast, the best managers are constantly operating at the leading edge of their responsibility spectrum and sometimes they are leaning over the boundaries, beyond their job description; they often feel empowered enough as not to ask anyone's permission. They experiment, regularly trying out new methods with their teammates. ***They push it.***

The effective and empowered leaders create an environment where everyone feels that is their obligation and authority to push the envelope. They accomplish this by surrounding themselves with the right people, get rid of the wrong ones and delegate or assign the right responsibilities to the right people. Also, effective managers make it clear to their associates that it is their responsibility to find their own room to roam. Effective leaders go the distance to make sure that the individual who takes the initiative is not made into a scapegoat should things go wrong. They try to learn from mistakes, understand what went wrong in the process, and encourage for a better result next time. Then they move on, without holding grudges.

All of the material presented herein was intended to assist managers in avoiding complacency and encourage them to think outside the box. They need to challenge the status quo, by answering first the question *"What needs to be done?"* and subsequently answering the *"What can and should I do to make a difference?"* question. These two are the questions that reflect responsibility, ownership, integrity and ultimately, **leadership.**

ACKNOWLEDGEMENTS

(*1) Robert Nickerson—Business and Information Systems; First Edition, Addison-Wesley, 1997.

(*2) Ron Kurtus—Ben Franklin's 13 Virtues (revised 7 February 2005), http://www.school-for-champions.com/character/franklin_virtues.htm

(*3) Jim Collins—Good to Great, First edition, HarperCollins books, 2001.

(*4) John Stuart Mill—System of Logic eight edition, 1872 http://www.utm.edu/research/iep/m/milljs.htm

(*5) Norman Vincent Peale (1898–1993) http://www.quotationspage. com/quotes/Norman_Vincent_Peale/

(*6) Gantt charts—www.ganttchart.com

(*7) Jack Griffin—How to Say It at Work, 1998.

(*8) Woopidoo! Business Quotations—http://www.woopidoo.com/business_quotes

(*9) Chris Jenkins—Be a "Person of Value" article, Harrington & Reed, Inc., 2004.

(*10) Abraham Maslow—Motivation and Personality, 2nd edition, Harper & Row, 1970.

(*11) Robert Gwynne—Maslow's Hierarchy of Needs, 1997

(*12) Dale Carnegie—How to Win Friends & Influence People, 1936; First Pocket Books Edition, 1982

(*13) Albert Mehrabian—Communication Research. www.businessballs.com/mehrabiancommunications.htm.

(*14) Nido Q.—How do you sound to others? http://hodu.com/speaking-skills.2.shtml.

(*15) Wertheim E. G.—The importance of effective communication. http://web.cba.neu.edu/~ewertheim/interper/commun.htm

(*16) Garza D, Becan-McBride K.—Phlebotomy Handbook: Blood Collection Essentials, phlebotomy practice and healthcare settings, 6th Ed. Upper Saddle River, NJ, Prentice Hall, 2002.

(*17) A Comparative Anthology of Sacred Texts— http://origin.org/ucs

(*18) Carley H. Dodd—Dynamics of Intercultural Communication, Fifth Edition, Mc Graw-Hill 1998

(*19) Stephen R. Covey—7 Habits of Highly Effective People, Simon and Schuster, 1989

(*20) Schermerhorn, Hunt, Osborn: Organizational Behavior, Eighth Edition, 2000

(*21) Viktor E. Frankl—Man's Search for Meaning, Beacon Press, 1984

(*22) Churchill anticipates the Battle of Britain—Sir Winston Churchill, Prime Minister of Great Britain's Speech Before the House of Commons, June 18, 1940; http://www.rjgeib.com/thoughts/britain/britain.html

(*23) Brainy Quote, http://www.brainyquote.com/quotes/authors/a/aristotle.html

(*24) Hout, TM & Carter, JC—Getting it done: new roles for senior executives. Harvard Business Review, 1995

(*25) Alfred P. Sloan Jr. quotations, http://www.creativequotations.com/one/1399a.htm

(*26) Michael E. Porter—Competitive Advantage, First Free Press edition, 1985

(*27) Robert A. Lutz—The Seven Laws of Business That Made Chrysler the World's Hottest Car Company, John Willey & Sons, New York 1998

(*28) Six Sigma Systems, http://www.sixsigmasystems.com/

(*29) Daniel E. O'Leary—Enterprise Resource Planning (ERP) Systems Course Page http://www.usc.edu/schools/business/atisp/ERP/

(*30) Enterprise Resource Planning—from Wikipedia, the free encyclopedia http://en.wikipedia.org/wiki/Enterprise_resource_planning

(*31) Orit Gadiesh, James L. Gilbert—Transforming Corner-Office Strategy into Frontline Action; Harvard Business Review Article May 1, 2001

(*32) Southwest Airlines Company—http://www.mba.tuck.dartmouth.edu/pdf/2002-2-0012.pdf

(*33) Phillip Kotler—Marketing Management, Prentice Hall, 11th edition, 2003

(*34) Oren Harari—The Leadership Secrets of Colin Powel, McGraw-Hill, 2002.

(*35) Time Management: Making the Most of a Limited Resource—Dale M. Johnson, Western Maryland Research and Education Center; James C. Hanson, Department of Agricultural and Resource Economics University of Maryland at College Park.

(*36) Robert A. Levin, Joseph G. Rosse—Talent Flow, First edition, Jossey-Bass 2001.

(*37) Philip Kotler—Marketing Management, Twelfth edition, Prentice Hall, 2005.

(*38) Lance A. Berger, Dorothy R. Berger—The Compensation Handbook, Fourth edition, McGraw-Hill, 1999.

(*39) Robert Slater—The GE Way Fieldbook: Jack Welch's Battle Plan for Corporate Revolution, McGraw-Hill, 2000

978-0-595-37540-0
0-595-37540-5